How to Have Kids with Character

(Even if Your Kids Are Characters)

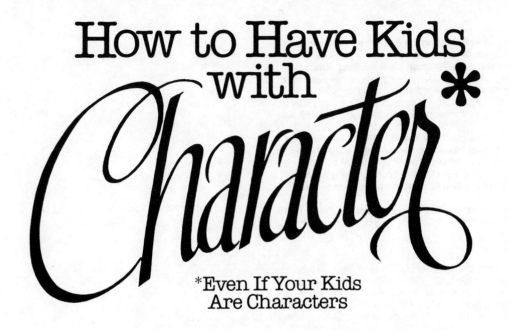

How to Have Kids with *Character*

*Even If Your Kids
Are Characters

NADINE M. BROWN

Tyndale House Publishers, Inc.
Wheaton, Illinois

AUTHOR'S NOTE

The original manuscript was written using the Authorized King James Version of the Bible for all Scripture references. This is my personal preference for reading and memorization because I feel the King James is unsurpassed in its beauty of English poetry and prose. It can also have the advantage of providing a lifelong word-key to major concordances, which will assist your children later as they search for Scriptures they memorized as a child. For these reasons, I encourage you to use it with your child.

The use of other translations (primarily The New King James Version of the Bible) is a decision of the publishers in an attempt to make the verses easier for younger children to understand and memorize. Also, an appendix of Scriptures is included at the end of this book, showing the main verses in two other translations: The New International Version and *The Living Bible.*

Finally, Tyndale House Publishers has been gracious in providing additional artwork in the text. In a number of cases, they chose the design and subject matter.

Scripture quotations are from *The Holy Bible,* The New King James Version (NKJV), copyright © 1979, 1980, 1982 by Thomas Nelson Inc., Publishers, unless otherwise indicated as being from: *The Holy Bible,* The King James Version (KJV), *The Holy Bible,* The New International Version (NIV), copyright © 1973, 1978, 1984 by International Bible Society. Used by permission of Zondervan Bible Publishers; or from *The Living Bible,* copyright © 1971 owned by assignment by Illinois Regional Bank N.A. (as trustee), all rights reserved.

Cover and interior art by Ron Wheeler

Library of Congress Catalog Card Number 89-51647
ISBN 0-8423-1607-8
Copyright © 1990 by Nadine M. Brown
All rights reserved
Printed in the United States of America

96 95 94 93 92 91 90
9 8 7 6 5 4 3 2

Dedicated to my parents, Earl and Opal Maynard, whose diligence to lovingly guide and correct their four children provided me with a wonderful Christian heritage; and to my two sons, Philip and Nathan, whose questions on how to teach character qualities to their children provided the impetus for writing this book.

ACKNOWLEDGMENTS

I wish to express my heartfelt appreciation to my husband, Allan Brown, for sharing my deep concern and interest in our sons' development. His hours of patient training have been invaluable in the maturing of our sons' Christian character.

Special thanks are due to Philip and Nathan, whose willingness to assume household chores during the writing of this manuscript made its publication possible.

And to Mrs. LaVonne Striffler, an enthusiastic Christian friend, who was most helpful in checking the original manuscript for syntax and spelling errors. Her assistance was sincerely appreciated.

Contents

Introduction

"Mom, see how tall I am now!"

"I'm almost as tall as you are, Dad!"

We listen to the tiptoed claims of our children and at intervals add a new mark to the growth chart on the wall behind the door.

It seems so easy. The days and months go by and new inches of growth are added. How delightful it would be if we could check off certain character traits in addition to the inches. Think of it, by the time a child reaches thirty-six inches he would have a good foundation in obedience. And, with the coming months and inches, dependability, honesty, and responsibility would follow.

There are certain character qualities we all want for our children. We want them to learn to obey, to finish a job, to be honest even when it hurts, and to be self-controlled. Yet we often are unsure how to help our children learn these things.

My odyssey to learn about character qualities began one day when I was a pre-teen—the day I realized that children do not always become the teenagers their parents expect them to become. I was sitting in one of those large, comfortably cushioned, canopied yard swings in the California twilight. My parents were renewing friendships with college friends who had recently returned from a missionary tour in the Far East. We children, ten through fourteen, were left to make acquaintance with each other as best we could.

That evening in the yard swing, I listened as the missionaries' daughter, Mona, entertained my sister and me with her escapades. She told of lying to her parents to attend parties, and of wild car rides through the streets on some boy's lap.

Whether Mona added spice to her stories to impress her junior audience, I don't know. But from that day on I faced child rearing with a premature trepidation. And I became interested in learning how a parent could develop in children those character qualities that they wanted to see blossom in their teen years. Eventually I came to realize that perhaps what parents need to do is plan ways to develop character qualities, just as they often plan menus each day for breakfast, lunch, or dinner!

So, if you are among those parents who want their children to develop biblical character qualities, yet you haven't been sure how to go about doing it, this book is for you. Twelve character qualities are presented in this book, one for each month of the year. There also are activities for each character quality. You can take the qualities in sequence, or pick and choose as you feel the need. In this way, you don't have to read the whole book at once. (Besides, when have you read a book all the way through uninterrupted in the last five years?) By taking only a few minutes at the beginning of the month, you will be able to plan for the days ahead. One note: Be sure to include your children in the planning. Children love a challenge and generally will respond better to improvements when they have helped plan them.

Each chapter includes a definition of the character quality (which is simple enough to be learned by a toddler); short, catchy phrases to help children keep the character quality in mind; Scripture references that can be copied by your youngsters and taped to the refrigerator or put on their bulletin board; and suggestions for practical, age-related activities to include character-quality training in your daily routine.

If your children are small (two to seven years old), you may want to begin in Chapter 1 and work through a chapter a month. If your children are older (eight to fourteen years old) and you need immediate help, you may want to begin with the chapter on obedience (Chapter 3). Then choose chapters at random throughout the book, depending on which quality your children seem to need the most.

One thing to keep in mind: the closer your children are to the teen years the more you need to present character development as something *they* are working on and you are simply helping them with. When you first start working on character qualities, older children may squirm and squawk. (Many seem to think that is how they are supposed to respond!) But most teens soon feel a great deal of quiet relief knowing that, after all, you are aware of the big responsibilities they will soon be taking on in adulthood—and are working to help them learn ways to deal with those responsibilities.

Chapter One. Perseverance:
Finishing What I Start

"I want to do it! I want to do it! Let me do it!" begged Philip, more times than I could count.

So I'd hand over the mixing bowl or pull a chair up to the soapy dishwater for him. Two minutes later I'd turn around, and my willing helper would have disappeared!

Because children get distracted or lose interest in activities so easily, we know we will have plenty of opportunities to teach the character quality of perseverance. A simple definition for this big word is, "Finishing what I started to do."

My husband and I found mealtime an ideal opportunity for teaching our sons to finish what they started. When we served the children's plates, we gave them small helpings with the stipulation that they had to eat it all.

So there they sat with that mountainous obstacle of five peas in front of them. Such a challenge usually called for reinforcements, so their glasses were refilled with milk. Then with glass in one hand, fork poised in the other, and a few grimaces, down the food would go. When that last pea disappeared off the plate, our young men knew they had accomplished something important.

These tactics led to some interesting habits. I recall the day Philip, then fifteen, looked at the traditional two slices of squash on his plate and asked, "Can't I have a bit more? I'm hungry!"

A few spoonfuls may seem unimportant, but character—like a monument—is built by one small accomplishment at a time. Jesus told us that he who was faithful in little things would be given greater responsibility. Your children will all too soon receive bigger responsibilities: a job, marriage, children to rear—and greatest of all, a call to commitment to Christ. Your job as a parent is to help them be ready to fulfill these responsibilities.

How disappointing it is to parents when their grown children haven't learned to persevere in one of these greater responsibilities.

"We can't understand it," I overheard an older couple complaining to friends in a restaurant. "We've stuck with our marriage for thirty-five years, but two of our four married children are divorced."

If we want our children to keep a job or stick with the adjustments of a difficult marriage, we need to teach them perseverance as early and as frequently as possible. Even busy moms and dads can remind a child, "We finish the job—so let's get that last mouthful down!"

Unfortunately, one of the big temptations for parents who desire to see improvement in their children is to try to change everything overnight. But the key to success is to work on one or two small improvements at a time, and to see that these are done consistently. This makes more sense than to hope for a complete character make-over in a month.

For example, talk about the character quality you are working on as many times a day as you find instances where it might fit. Then leave the application of the principle to your child. It has been amazing

We can keep at the task of training when we realize our children's character development is more important than getting a job done quickly.

to me to watch my children transfer the "finish-the-job" concept to other areas after we worked on it at the dinner table.

I recall a particularly trying meal, with peas tucked under the edge of the plate and potatoes spread all across it. (In a child's mind, spreading food around a bit makes it look like it's eaten.) I rescued the peas from their hiding place and scraped the potatoes together again. Finally, though, the boys finished their food. As they went off to play, I cleaned the table and wondered if child rearing was really worth the effort.

A bit later Nathan called from his room, "Come on, Mom. Come and see!" I wearily dropped the dishrag and went to "see." He stood in the doorway of his room, beaming. All his toys were put away and he announced, "See, I finished the job."

So hang in there, Mom and Dad. And remember, you need to persevere, too, as you try to teach this character quality to your children.

SCRIPTURE

Here is a good Scripture to use in teaching your child perseverance:

"A desire accomplished is sweet to the soul" (Proverbs 13:19).

Write this Scripture on construction paper and hang it in a prominent place for a month. Let your children find pictures of their favorite "sweets" to decorate the page. The more you involve your youngsters in active projects to learn a character quality, the more important that character quality will be to them.

When you assign your child a task—such as making the bed or picking up all the blocks—and he finally finishes it, have him stand in the doorway with you to survey the room (or corner, if that is all he's managed!).

Many a time Philip or Nathan and I have stood looking at a straightened sock drawer or a picked up floor. "Doesn't it feel good when you finally get the job done?" I'd ask. Then I'd brag, "Boy, that looks nice!" or "You sure did finish the job!" Enthusiastic praise for your child's small accomplishments help make the work worth the effort. Though they may not be aware of it, the sense of inner satisfaction that results from your praise often will keep them working on a job when you aren't watching. This satisfaction can prompt them to get up on time and even try to make the bed without you reminding them. Your encouragement and praise when your children are young may well be what helps motivate them through high school and even beyond, when there may be no one around to praise them for their accomplishments.

Some children find it hard to persevere because they don't see any value in doing their chores. One of our children decided at an early age that he did not like work. By the time he was six, his goal in life was to avoid work as much as possible.

You, too, may have a child who is developing such a philosophy of life. Here are some special tactics my husband and I found helpful in working with such youngsters:

1. Talk to your children about how much they enjoy playing after chores are done. Compare this feeling with the boredom they feel when they have nothing to do.

2. Explain to them that God planned work for man as soon as he created him. Adam was to tend the Garden of Eden and dress the plants. So work was not intended to be a punishment. Rather, it is a source of feelings of accomplishment and satisfaction.

3. Tie some big words that communicate maturity and being grown-up to doing work. Telling a child it is important (or "impressive," "significant," "superior," "paramount," "outstanding," or whatever) to finish the job can give him a personal sense of importance.

*T*he key to success is working on one or two improvements at a time and seeing that they are done consistently.

4. Be sure to give your children several opportunities to finish small tasks and get big praise. This helps them develop an inner sense of satisfaction in work that has been completed.

Believe me, it does pay off! I knew we were beginning to change our work-avoiding son's attitude when he announced one day, "You know, work's not so bad. It makes play so much more fun!"

SLOGANS

Here are four short slogans to use when you are teaching your child the character quality of perseverance. You can use a new one each week of the month:

- Do a Proud Job.
- A Job Worth Doing Is Worth Doing Well.

- Finish the Job.
- I Can Do It, God Will Help Me.

You or your children can write these slogans out on construction paper and put them on a bulletin board, the refrigerator, or a wall.

You may want to enhance a slogan different ways. Children love picture taking, so at the beginning of the month (and at the end of a roll of film!), take a picture of your child beside his neat bed or toy shelf. Have the picture blown up to 5″ x 7″ size, then paste it on construction paper. If your child is old enough, let him write "I finish the job" below the picture. Finally, be sure to hang it in a prominent place where friends and family can add their praise and encouragement as the child learns about perseverance.

Sometime between the ages of two and three youngsters begin that emphatic announcement: "I can do it!" So take advantage of this stage and let them try to button a sweater or fold a washcloth. Even if the task seems difficult for your child, resist the temptation to do it for him. Instead, show your child how to do the task (i.e., get his fingers behind a button and push it through the buttonhole) and then let him work at it until he accomplishes it.

One thing to note: I have qualified the slogan "I can do it" by adding "God will help me." As I prepared this book, one character quality I looked for in Proverbs was independence. I wanted to teach it to my children. But I was surprised to discover the concept of independence wasn't there! Instead, Scripture emphasized that children are to look to parents for guidance and help, and eventually to transfer their dependence to God. True, we can do all things—but we can do them *through* Christ, who strengthens us.

ACTIVITIES

Two to Seven Years Old

In these early years, children enthusiastically offer to help with any task that looks interesting. They want to paint, mow the lawn, or run the vacuum—at least for five minutes. (Interest in painting seems to last longer than interest in other things. There is so much more scope for disaster here!) But their interest in most activities evaporates as soon as the fun becomes work.

When your children volunteer to help on a big job, accept their offer with limits. For example, if a child is just six years old, assign him two strips of the lawn to mow or a two-foot square of the garden next to you to weed. Then, when he has finished the task, he is free to move on or to ask for another small, limited assignment.

It is easier and faster to finish a task for our children, but that won't teach them to finish the job for themselves.

If you don't set limits and if you seem relieved when your children lose interest and wander away, you are teaching them to work only as long as work is fun. By setting specific limits to your children's part of a task, they can learn to finish the job at an early age.

Keep in mind, however, that you need to supervise your children at this stage. It was easy for me to tell the boys to get their pajamas on or brush their teeth, then get busy with my work and forget to see the chore was carried out. At these times, I found that a timer was a wonderful help to me. After I'd given an assignment, I would set the timer to remind myself to check on their progress.

Here are some suggested activities for teaching perseverance to this age group. Have your children:

1. Clean their plates at mealtime (small helpings, please!).
2. Fold and put away their pajamas each morning when they get up.
3. Put away their own toys—ages two to four will need your help, inspiration, and encouragement. One

thing to consider about this task: If you find that you often allow the toys to get knee-deep in your children's room before you make them pick things up, your first step in this perseverance project may be to require the children to put away one set of toys before they can get out another. (But if you do start out this way, be sure to concentrate on that chore for a week or two, until they are used to doing it.)

4. Put on their own shoes.

5. Tie their own shoes (five- to seven-year-olds).

Eight to Fifteen Years Old

Your goal during these years of your children's lives is to teach them to finish tasks without being reminded all the time and to evaluate their own work.

A friend of mine told me about a time when she asked her ten-year-old to clean his room. He shot into his room and out again like he'd gone through a revolving door. She knew there was no way he could be done so quickly, so she sent him back in.

Two minutes later he was outside playing again. This time they both went to check on the room. As they stood in the doorway surveying the semi-disaster she asked, "Do you call this clean?"

"Looks clean to me," was his stout reply.

"Well, we're having company tomorrow, and they are going to sleep in here," she announced.

He took one shocked look around and asked, "In this mess?"

Finishing a job and doing it well is a matter of perspective, and you want your children to develop a mature perspective. Children learn to evaluate work several ways. Here are some specific activities for this area:

1. After you have cleaned a room, bring your children in and ask them if you have done a good job. For example, if you've cleaned the bathroom, point out how the towels are folded and straight on the towel rod. Have them look in the sink to see that all the telltale rings are gone. Hold up the soap dish so they can see what a clean one looks like. Let them know what kinds of things they need to check when they do a job.

2. When your children ask you to check their work for them, find three or four things they did well so you can compliment them before pointing out any lacks or mistakes. ("Good, you have picked up all the books; now you just need to stand them up straight on the bookshelf.").

3. Give your children opportunities to evaluate their work before you do. Explain to them that soon they will be grown and will be the ones to decide whether they have done a good job or not.

If you are relieved when your children lose interest in helping you and wander away, you are teaching them to work only as long as work is fun, rather than to work until a job is finished.

At ten years of age, Nathan would mow the main part of the front yard when he was told to do it. But more often than not, he forgot the eight-foot strip on the other side of the driveway, though it was obviously out front. By the time he was twelve, he managed to remember both sections of the front yard, but had to be told when it needed to be cut. However, Philip, his sixteen-year-old brother, kept his own check on the back yard and needed few reminders to see that it was kept cut. These character qualities will come in time, if you just keep working on them.

Other activities for this age group include having them:

1. Weed a section of the yard, trim edges of the grass, or mow the lawn. (If your children are eight to eleven years old, have them work together on this.)

2. Fold clothes while listening to a tape or story. (I found this a good deterrent for boys who thought the laundry hamper was a magical way to get rid of clothes, even clean ones, that they didn't want to hang up.)

3. Set the table, wash dishes, or help clear off the table nightly.
4. Arrange a bookcase.
5. Straighten clothing drawers.

SOME CAUTIONS

There are a few things you need to be aware of when you start these projects.

1. Working with children is often frustrating, especially since we can do most tasks faster ourselves. But remember, your children's development is more important than any task. So resist the temptation to do things for them. Let them learn to finish the job themselves.

2. Don't give your children tasks that are beyond their abilities. This defeats your purpose and makes it impossible for them to learn to finish the job.

3. Be a good example. Be sure you finish hobby projects, cleaning, or other tasks you start. Many people find it easy to be hard with others, but so difficult to discipline themselves. It could be that you need to mature in this character quality, too. If so, let this be a time when you and your children can grow together.

Chapter Two. Honesty:
Telling the Truth, Even When It Hurts

I was having trouble with Nathan not telling the truth. When I asked questions such as, "Who didn't finish drinking all his milk?" I had the nagging feeling that he wasn't always honest in his answers. But I didn't know for sure. This problem had gone on for some months, and I was frustrated. Finally I asked the Lord to help me deal with it.

At lunch that day, Nathan had a peanut butter sandwich. He wasn't eating the crusts, so I reminded him to be sure to do so. Then I got busy working in another room. The next thing I knew the door slammed, and he had gone out to play.

In the kitchen I checked the table. Sure enough, the sandwich was gone, crusts and all. "What a good kid!" I thought, smiling to myself.

Then I stopped short. Maybe this was too good to be true!

I checked the sink—nothing. Under the table—nothing. Then I thought to check the pull-out trash can. There were the crusts, right on top!

Now maybe being concerned about whether or not my kids eat the crusts is a carry-over from my childhood; maybe no one eats them anymore. But honesty is always important—yesterday, today, and forever. So I breathed a prayer of "Thank you, Lord!" for now I had a better idea how to handle the situation. I went outside to where my son was playing and asked him a few questions.

"You ate all your sandwich, huh?"

"Yes."

"Did you throw any away?"

"Nope!"

"Are you sure you didn't put the crusts in the trash?"

"No!"

"Okay, come with me," I said taking Nathan's hand, and we walked into the house together and pulled out the trash can.

There lay the evidence!

That's how I discovered the honest check of asking questions when you already know the answers. And that incident still comes to Nathan's mind when he hears about a child who tells lies. "I know what to do with a kid like that," he says. "I can still remember standing looking at those bread crusts!" It was a turning point for him in accepting and acknowledging the truth.

Ask the Lord to help you be sensitive to your children and alert for hints of dishonesty. Children need incidents like the one with the bread crusts during their growing-up years so they know they can't get away with telling lies.

SCRIPTURE
The Bible has a great deal to say about honesty. Here are four Scriptures your children should learn as you emphasize this character quality this month:

One way to check honesty is to ask some questions when you already know the answers.

"Be sure your sin will find you out" (Numbers 32:23).

"If a ruler [or parent] pays attention to [believes] lies, All his servants [children] become wicked" (Proverbs 29:12).

"He who covers his sins will not prosper, but whoever confesses and forsakes them will have mercy" (Proverbs 28:13).

"Lying lips are an abomination to the Lord, but those who deal truthfully are his delight" (Proverbs 12:22).

There are several Bible stories that illustrate the principle of the first Scripture. You may want to include them in your family devotions this month. One such story, the story of Achan, is found in Judges 6 and 7. In sharing this story, you can point out that lying has an effect on those around us as well as on ourselves.

In Acts 5 we read of Ananias and Sapphira, two people who wanted to appear generous and important in the eyes of their church friends. In their church, many members sold land and gave all the profit to the apostles. However, though Ananias and Sapphira wanted to look just as generous as anyone else, they didn't want to give away all the money they made from selling their property. They seemed to think God wouldn't know how much money they had received, so they lied about their profits. And they paid for that lie. This story can be used to help your children understand that even if no one else finds out about a lie, God always knows.

The second Scripture verse from Proverbs 29 reminds me of a family in the church where I grew up. They seemed genuinely concerned about serving God, so as a young person I couldn't understand why none of their four children were interested in being Christians. Then one evening while visiting their home, I overheard teenaged Kristi, the oldest girl, warning her brother, "If you don't lie to Mom for me about last night, I won't lie for you this weekend."

I don't know just what went wrong in this family, but it seems that years ago the parents began believing their children's lies. To this day, none of the children are Christians.

In our society, we discourage children from telling about disobedience they see. We have tagged the name "tattle-tale" to our informers. What we ought to do is thank them and check into the situation.

Over the years my husband and I have asked Sunday school teachers, school teachers, and other adults to keep us informed of our boys' activities. I know our children well enough to know they get into mischief when they are out of my sight. That's only normal. And you can be sure yours will, too. If any adult cares enough about your child—and respects you enough—to tell you of your child's misdeeds, you should be grateful, not resentful.

The third Scripture, Proverbs 28:13, illustrates that where the letter of the law kills, mercy plays a beautiful role. If a child does admit wrongdoing and is truly sorry for what he has done, you may want to lighten or omit punishment. There is no virtue in undue harshness. We all need mercy from God, and we should be as willing to give it as we are to receive it.

However, you will need wisdom here to detect when the "Yes, I did it" admissions are flippant escapes from correction. Through you, your children can learn that God is both a God of justice and a God of mercy. They must see both sides of him if you ever hope that God will be their friend.

The final Scripture verse gives—in a nutshell, so to speak—a balanced view of God. The things that are an abomination to him are contrasted with the things that delight him. Encourage your children to be honest, explaining that this pleases the Father who loves them more than they can imagine.

Also, as you prepare to teach your children honesty be sure to make it a special matter of prayer. Ask God to give you insight into your children's thoughts and actions. Such special insights have been very helpful to us through the years.

SLOGANS

Here are four short slogans for the character quality of honesty. You can use a new one each week of the month:

- Honesty Is the Best Policy.
- Dishonesty Doesn't Pay.
- A Man (Child) Is Only As Good As His Word.
- To Thine Own Self Be True—Honesty to Others Will Follow.

The last slogan is an especially important one. You need to teach your children to balance truth, and to be honest in their thoughts about themselves.

Just yesterday Nathan, our thirteen-year-old, and I were looking at his last report card. His conduct had dropped from an "A" to a "B." I was curious why.

"Well, you see," he began to explain, "The other kids pick on me and when I do something back I always get caught but they never do!" (Sound familiar?) Then he entered into a pity party over the grave injustices of life.

I sat listening a while, then couldn't help but respond, "You know, Nathan, I'm sure there are times you get in trouble when someone else is at fault. But think of the dozens of times *you* are up to mischief and don't get caught!"

He tried to fight it, but the smile tugging at the corners of his mouth won. He burst into laughter, recalling some escapade from which he had recently emerged unscathed. But this incident helped Nathan recognize the truth about his circumstances. Yes, he sometimes bore the brunt of another child's actions. But there also were times that he went unpunished though he was far from innocent.

One note about honesty, the pages of history are a great source of valuable lessons that you can share with your children. Consider stories like Abraham Lincoln walking miles to return money that wasn't his, or George Washington's confession when he cut down the cherry tree. Your local library should have children's stories on the lives of these men.

ACTIVITIES

Two to Seven Years Old
The three most common concerns of parents with small children are:
  1. How can I tell if my child is telling the truth?
  2. How can I tell if my child knows when he is lying or understands what telling the truth is all about?
  3. What do I do with a child who will not admit he has lied—even when he is caught?

When you stand with little Ryan in front of the "cave drawings" recently added to the living room wall and ask, "Did you do that?" the poor kid is on the horns of a dilemma. Your tone of voice and facial expression hardly give him hope of a reward for his artistic efforts. If he says "yes," the sky may fall. The only other possibility is "no" (though there are some little jewels who consider "I don't know" a viable option).

Even if crayon is in hand, your child is sure he couldn't have done anything to make you so upset. The result of course is, "No, I didn't do it!"

It is very natural for children at this age to tell you what they think you want to hear. They really do

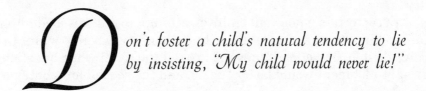

Don't foster a child's natural tendency to lie by insisting, "My child would never lie!"

want to please you. Once the words are spoken the child begins to believe them, whether they mirror reality or not.

There are some specific things you can do to discover the answers to the three questions listed above:

1. Ask questions you know the answers to. Pay careful attention to how your child responds. Note how much eye shifting, expression changing, and squirming occurs.

These can be simple questions to begin with, questions your children have no difficulty answering. When you know your daughter has eaten all her cereal and gone out to play, ask her whether she ate all her breakfast. Compare her light-hearted, easy response to the response you get at other times.

2. Ask your children questions about non-threatening situations, situations when they haven't done anything wrong but you are just seeing how they will respond. Be sure to tell them right up front, "You're not in any trouble, but I was wondering. . . ."

Some parents have the mistaken idea that quizzing children makes them lie. Quite to the contrary, quizzing them reveals what they choose to say, but doesn't make them say anything! When done appropriately, either in a non-threatening or straightforward manner depending on the situation, quizzing children can be a very helpful tool for both child and parent.

3. Encourage trustworthiness in your children by complimenting their honesty any time they exhibit it, even for the simplest answers if they are accurate, honest ones. This will help your child focus on the importance of honesty.

4. Consider giving extra correction when your children attempt to hide disobedience. As soon as the boys were old enough to understand, their father let them know honesty was important to him. In fact, he told them they would receive double correction if they did not tell the truth when questioned about something they had done. The first punishment would be for the lie, and the second for whatever they were trying to hide.

5. Resist the temptation to entertain friends or family with recountings of your children's dishonest or disrespectful antics, especially in the child's presence. It's true that youngsters can say and do some very amusing things. But God warns us in Proverbs 14:9 that a person who makes jokes about sin is a fool. What seems funny from a child of three won't be the least bit funny from a youth of thirteen.

6. Realize that children have a natural tendency toward deceit and avoid fostering that tendency by insisting, "My child would never lie!" All children tell less than the whole truth at times. We must help them know the difference between the truth and lies, and teach them to be willing to tell the truth even when it hurts.

7. Be an example for your children. Be honest and straightforward with them and with others. Your children learn most effectively from seeing how you react and behave with them and with others.

Eight to Fifteen Years Old
1. We all have a strong tendency to explain situations in a way that puts us in the best possible light.

They don't teach us this in kindergarten, so it must come naturally. When a child's explanation puts all the blame on a brother's or sister's doorstep, you can be pretty sure it deserves a second look. It may be accurate, but then again it may not.

Think creatively as you listen to your children. "Mommy, my brother won't play with me," can mean "We were playing and I chose all the best cars, now he won't play." Or, "All I did was hit him on the head

If you check up on your kids from time to time, you may find there is very little need. But if you don't, you may be in for a sad surprise.

and now he is walking off." Or, "I quit. But now I want to play again and he won't." Be tuned in to what is missing from a story, as well as what is included.

The other evening one of our boys returned from a youth Bible study. When my husband asked how things had gone, he received a glowing report. "There was just something about it," Allan told me later, "that reminded me of how I used to report to my mom. Especially if something had happened I knew she wouldn't approve of. So I began to question further. 'Who was there?' 'What did they talk about?' Sure enough there was a lot I needed to know lying beneath the surface of that first glossy report!"

2. If the Lord flashes a caution light in your mind, check into the stories your children are telling you. If your daughter said she was going to the library after school today, but for some reason you are sure she isn't there, give the library a call to find out. Checking up on your kids from time to time can show you there is very little need to do so. But it can also let you know when there is a potential problem—hopefully before it is too serious.

Our oldest son related an interesting incident recently. One of his classmates drove to high school daily and his stepfather had been admonishing ("bugging," in his classmates' words) him about his driving. The boy had insisted he wasn't doing anything wrong, but the father had reason to believe this wasn't true. On this particular morning, the father had followed his stepson to school—and clocked him doing 70 MPH in a 55 MPH zone! The kid was fit to be tied.

"You know," Philip chuckled, "David is lucky. He has a smart dad who cares enough about him to check up on him."

3. Begin early letting your children know that future privileges depend on present honesty and dependability. Permission granted can be prefaced by, "Because I know you have always been honest, I will let you go. But remember if I ever find you are not where you said you would be—boy, oh boy, will you miss out on a lot of activities!"

4. You must be honest as well and follow through with the promised correction or withhold privileges that have been forfeited. If you are not honest and do not keep your word, you short-circuit the whole process. Perhaps the worst part is that your children will not appreciate you for not carrying through on what you have said. Generally, they actually think less of you and of themselves when they are not held to a high standard.

5. Never ignore dishonesty when you know your children are shading the truth. Deceitfulness becomes a way of life that can plague your children and those around them through the teen years and on into marriage. One young lady who had been married only two years lamented, "I don't know what to do. My husband lies to me frequently about where he is going and who he is with. He says he used to lie to his parents all the time." Don't let your children get away with something that can only cause them harm.

6. Teach your children to be honest when telling about their own actions. When you call your children in to explain a disagreement, make them talk one at a time—and **no** interruptions allowed. When one is all finished, then the other may talk. Don't let responses to questions like, "What did you do?" begin with, "Well, see, she. . . !" Insist on hearing what each child did from that child. Let each one speak for herself.

MAKE BED ✓
CLEAN ROOM ✓
HOMEWORK
WRITE GRANDMA.
SWEEP GARAGE
MOW LAWN

Chapter Three. Obedience: *Doing What I Am Told, When I Am Told, with a Good Attitude*

Obedience! Can you really get it from a child?

If the only responsibility we parents had in life was seeing that our children were obedient, I'm sure we could all do a pretty good job. But we are busy earning a living, sweeping the garage, fixing dinner, cleaning the floor, and a multitude of other things. In the meantime our children spend all of five years (and the better part of ten) seeing if we are going to make them mind or if they can have their own way.

Willing obedience is probably the most important character quality you will develop in your child. In many ways, it is the foundation upon which everything else is built.

Suppose you and the children were spending a quiet evening at home. After half an hour or so, it seemed just too quiet! So, you decided to check on the kids.

The first bedroom was empty. The door to the second one was closed. You opened the door quietly, and the room was dark. For a moment you thought no one was there either. Then you realized a candle was glowing on the other side of the bed, and you could just make out three children sitting around it. As you listened, you realized they were trying to have a séance!

Do you react as strongly to the scene I have just described as you would to your child telling you "No!" or obeying with a rebellious attitude?

Did you know that God says disobedience or rebellion is comparable to the sin of witchcraft? (1 Samuel 15:23).

A person involved in witchcraft has aligned himself with Satan and follows his suggestions. And Satan's very first suggestion to man was to disobey God and ignore his authority. Even today, his most common suggestion is for people of any age to rebel against the authorities God has placed in their lives.

Most parents wouldn't think of letting their children be involved in witchcraft or play with a Ouija board. What they don't realize is that when they ignore childish defiance and rebellion they are permitting an alliance with evil.

It may seem a bit melodramatic to compare a child's rebellion to witchcraft. When children are small, it's easy to handle or ignore their disobedience. But if you have ever lived with a full-blown, rebellious teenager, you will appreciate the comparison.

I had that experience during my own teen years. One of my brothers rebelled against our parents' authority. He decided at fifteen that he was going to quit school and do what he wanted, when he wanted, and they had better get out of his way. His sullen countenance mirrored his anger at the world and everyone in it. The tension and antagonism that filled our home made life miserable for everyone. That experience had a profound impact on my own concern about rearing children.

If the purpose of obedience was just to please parents, it wouldn't be so important. But obedience to parents is only the training ground for a child's later obedience to God's guidance. How can a child who has made a million self-willed, rebellious decisions before he is twelve years old submit to God's leadership when he is older?

But be encouraged, Dad and Mom—you *can* have obedient children, as long as you are willing to train them for obedience. I can assure you, it is well worth the effort. As Proverbs 15:20 says, "A wise son makes a father [and mother] glad."

So, how do you train your children to obey proper authority? The book of Deuteronomy gives some excellent guidelines for conducting a training program:

> *These words which I command thee this day*
> *shall be in thine heart:*
> *And thou shalt teach them diligently unto thy children,*
> *and shalt talk of them when thou sittest in thine house,*
> *and when thou walkest by the way,*
> *and when thou liest down and when thou risest up.*
> *(Deuteronomy 6:6-7, KJV).*

Notice the two-step sequence necessary for training. First, biblical principles must be in our hearts. We are to guide our lives by God's precepts and to give him joyful obedience. God wants us to have the richest, fullest life possible. This is a truth we should be sharing often with our children. We must believe that God's wisdom is vastly superior to ours, and that we could never improve on his instructions.

Second, we must train our children diligently. This means giving their training constant and persistent attention. We are to train them when we rise up in the morning, when we go to bed at night, when we are at home, or when we are out traveling.

The foundation of this training is communication. We are to talk to our children, telling them that God wants the very best for their lives. We are to tell them of his guidelines for living, letting them know they must be obedient because God has commanded it (Ephesians 6:1). (If communication is an area of difficulty for you, Chapter 10 may help you learn as well as teach new skills in this area.)

So we need to talk to our children about the importance of obedience when we drive them to school in the morning, when we sit at the dinner table, when we put them to bed at night—and every time in-between that we can think of it!

This sounds like a lot of work, doesn't it? But I assure you it becomes easier as you ask for God's help and let it become a habit.

If you have passed the first hurdle and are convinced that teaching your children to do what you say, when you say it, with a good attitude is God's standard, you're ready to start training your children to be obedient.

I know that in this day of instant everything, from coffee to potatoes, we want a magic cure for disobedience. I can't promise you that, but I can guarantee impressive results in three days of diligent training. And the more disobedient your children have been, the more amazing the results will be.

What will cause this wonderful change? The following three-day test.

First, you must prepare for the test by confessing to God your lack of diligent, consistent training. Ask his forgiveness for all the times you were too busy to stop and correct your children. Next, ask God to help you obey him in diligently training your children. The role of prayer cannot be overemphasized—it is your greatest source of help!

If the problem with your child is an especially difficult one, consider fasting. When our youngest was about nine, he had such a spirit of resistance to anything spiritual that I was very troubled. I had prayed for him often, but it seemed there was a barrier there even as I prayed. Almost as if Satan was saying, "Go ahead and pray, it won't do any good, he is not going to be a Christian!"

Finally I shared my concern with a friend who lived miles away. She encouraged me to fast and pray, and agreed to fast one meal a week with my husband and me. Since Jesus had said that some things only happen by prayer and fasting (Mark 9:29), I was willing.

If Children are to obey God they need to learn that he wants the very best for their lives.

This was in February. At Easter that year God really touched my son's heart. On the way home from church that day he shared with us, "Dad and Mom, I have never told you this, but there has always been a barrier between me and God." From that point on we have seen a continued opening of his heart to the Lord and to spiritual things. Fasting one meal a week has become a part of my dependence on God for wisdom in training my boys. I have shared the importance of this weapon of spiritual warfare with young couples in our congregation, and it has been a joy to hear their testimonies of the help they have found in training their children. Yes, we can do all things, but it is through Christ who strengthens us.

Second, you need to have a talk with your children. They of all people know just how careless and inconsistent you have been. You need to ask their forgiveness for your failure to obey God in rearing them.

This is one of the most important steps you will take, Dad and Mom, so don't bypass it.

I recall a young woman telling me of her rebellious teenage years. She had hardened her heart against her parents' scolding and correction. Then, one day during her senior year of high school, her father came into her room and with tears asked her forgiveness for his failures as a parent.

She said, "When he did that, all my defenses crumbled. I was prepared to resist his complaining, but I couldn't resist his confession and tears."

Does confessing your mistakes and failures to your children sound a bit scary? It should, because it puts you in a position of accountability. After I did this, my children began helping me be consistent. They would remind me if I was getting careless (especially if I was careless in disciplining one of the other children!).

Third, ask your children to help you pray. Tell them you want to obey God and to train them for obedience. After all, you are doing it for their good and you are all in this together.

Now you are ready to begin the three-day test. Choose three days when you will be together most of the time and when you don't have other major projects planned. These days should immediately follow your confession to your children and your request for their help.

On the morning of the first day, begin by explaining to your children what the guidelines are going to be. Tell them something like this: "I will speak to you once, at the most twice, so I am sure I have your attention. Then you are to put down what you are doing and mind me."

Explain that with God's help you are going to see that they come when they are called, that they will put away toys when they are told to, and that you will take up the switch and paddle them if they do not. It may be just one or two swats, but it must be consistently administered.

Were you afraid this was coming?

God tells us that talking to our children and explaining guidelines is crucial. Modern child psychology has emphasized this aspect of training, yet it often actively opposes God's instructions for punishment. Criticism by present-day psychologists and the increased focus on child abuse has made even Christian parents hesitant to obey God's guidelines and spank their children. Be assured that if you consistently, patiently, and lovingly correct your children you will not abuse them because you will be less likely to get angry with them. And if you do get angry, it is less likely that your anger will get out of control. More often than not, a consistent lack of discipline leads to childish rebellion, and it is this that can cause parents to become angry to the point that they discipline their children harshly.

Let's look at two modern approaches to raising children.

First, *Never spank your children*. Have you ever heard a parent lament, "But I love my child, I just can't spank him!" God says, "He who spares his rod hates his son, but he who loves him disciplines him promptly" (Proverbs 13:24). In Proverbs 23:13-14 we read, "Do not withhold correction from a child. For if

*P*ray that you will discipline your children consistently.
Ask them to pray for the same thing.
After all, you are in this together.

you beat him with a rod, he will not die. You shall beat him with a rod and deliver his soul from hell."

Too often it is not love for a child that keeps us from consistently applying discipline. It is self-love or laziness. Many parents simply don't want to endure the pain of spanking their children when they need it. Or they are too lazy to train them consistently. Or, like Eli the priest (1 Samuel 2:29), parents honor their children above God and do not have the courage to discipline them.

We all know the chorus, "Jesus loves me this I know." But do you know what God says his love will do? "The Lord disciplines those he loves, and he punishes everyone he accepts as a son" (Hebrews 12:6, NIV). Love—both God's love and parental love—is willing to take up a switch and a paddle if needed.

Also, did you know that God was concerned enough about older, rebellious, disobedient children that he gave special instructions concerning them? Have you ever read the sentence that was to be passed on them? It is found in Deuteronomy 21:18-21:

If a man has a stubborn and rebellious son who will not obey the voice of his father or the voice of his mother, and who, when they have chastened him, will not heed them, then his father and his mother shall take hold of him and bring him out to the elders of his city, to the gate of his city. And they shall say to the elders of his city, "This son of ours is stubborn and rebellious; he will not obey our voice; he is a glutton, and a drunkard."

Then all the men of his city shall stone him to death with stones; so you shall put away the evil person from among you, and all Israel shall hear and fear.

Does that sound cruel?

I am afraid we have a lot of misplaced sympathy today! God is not cruel; he is loving, merciful, and just. But his focus of concern is for the innocent, not the guilty.

Do you understand why he gave these instructions? God said, "so you shall put away the evil . . . from among you." The Israelites were promised a society free from the devastating ills we struggle with today—if they obeyed God. His guidelines are always for the benefit and protection of his people. His love has caused him to spell them out.

Although we are not a nation directly under God's leadership as the Israelites were, these guidelines help us understand why we have so much evil in our land. If we accept the principles underlying God's instructions for disciplining our children, we can save ourselves from a great deal of heartache.

Ironically, sometimes those who are most opposed to corporal discipline are the first to blame God for the evil in the land. They ask, "If God is good, why are little children molested?" or "How can God let drunken drivers kill innocent people?" It isn't God who is responsible for these tragedies. Rather, he has told us how to rear children so the lands we live in would not be filled with violence. As a nation we have chosen to ignore God's wisdom, and tolerate evil and immorality. We can't do that and not suffer the consequences. How ironic that we ignore God's instructions and then blame him for our problems.

The second modern approach to disobedience is, *Don't spank—deprive.* This approach is typified by parents who say, "But must I really spank my child? Can't I just send him to his room?" I noticed a recent ladies' magazine article that encouraged this practice. One of the sub-headings in the article was "Don't Spank: Deprive."

God could just as easily have said, "Send your child to the tent when he disobeys you." Instead he said, "He who spares his rod hates his son, but he who loves him disciplines him promptly" (Proverbs 13:24).

He could have told us to walk off and ignore our disobedient children. Instead he said, "The rod and

O bedience with a good attitude is the foundation for the development of other character qualities.

reproof give wisdom, But a child left to himself brings shame to his mother" (Proverbs 29:15).

I must confess I do not know why God designed spanking as the way to curtail a child's rebellious spirit. Or why "blows that hurt cleanse away evil, as do stripes the inner depths of the heart" (Proverbs 20:30). I just know God said it, and he is all wise; and I have seen it work again and again.

It is interesting that these instructions of God's generate such violent reactions. We are living with the results of a "Don't spank: Deprive" generation, but we still won't accept God's wisdom. (Sadly, many of those who raise a hue and cry about spanking a child have not a qualm about taking the child's life before it is fully developed.)

This reaction to God's plan for correction hasn't just happened, I'm sure. Satan is always trying to get us to accept some plan other than God's. If he can get us sidetracked in training our children for obedience, he has gone a long way toward winning the battle for our children. Satan is a liar, and the first big lie he tells parents is, "You need not spank your child; he will not surely die."

Are you thinking what most parents think when they consider a commitment to consistent discipline for their children? I can remember sitting in quiet despair on my living room couch thinking, "If I do that, I will be spanking my child every five minutes all day long." It didn't happen, though! My children were smarter than that. (I am pretty sure your children are smarter than that, too!) When my sons realized I really was going to take up the switch and spank them each time they disobeyed, they began minding. Success in the area of obedience was as simple as correcting my children one more time than they disobeyed.

If you have tried to train your children for obedience, and are not satisfied with your success, let me encourage you to start at the task once again, and have as a goal correcting your child just one more time than she disobeys.

SCRIPTURE

Here is a different Scripture on obedience for each week in the month. You will want to put them up where your children can see them daily:

"Children, obey your parents in the Lord, for this is right" (Ephesians 6:1).

"Even a child is known by his deeds, By whether what he does is pure and right" (Proverbs 20:11).

"Obedience is far better than sacrifice. [God] is much more interested in your listening to him than in your offering. . . . For rebellion is as bad as the sin of witchcraft" (1 Samuel 15:22-23, TLB).

"Obey those who rule over you, and be submissive, for they watch out for your souls, as those who must give account. Let them do so with joy" (Hebrews 13:17).

Your children may already have learned some of these Scriptures. Many youngsters learn them in their pre-school years. The last verse is for older children. It was written to members of a local congregation, but its application fits all of us in all areas of Christian life.

Notice that the emphasis of these verses is for a child to obey for his own sake. Through obedience, a child builds his own reputation, for "even a child is known by his actions."

(Perhaps an extra word of caution is needed here for people in Christian work. While it's true that your children's behavior can profoundly affect your ministry, they need to do right because it is right—not because of what people will think of you.)

SLOGANS

Here are four slogans you can use as you teach your children about obedience:

- We All Have to Obey Someone.

I recall an evening years ago when we were gathered around the dinner table. Our boys were trying to get this concept of authority straight.

"We have to mind you, Dad, but you don't have to mind anyone, do you?" they asked.

"Yes," the explanation went. "At the college where I teach I have to do what Dr. Palm, the academic dean, tells me to do."

"But he doesn't have to mind anyone, does he?"

"Oh, yes, he must mind the vice president." And on up the academic ladder we went.

It was so discouraging to the boys to find that everyone had to obey someone. In the back of their minds was the hope that someday they would be their own boss.

- You Can't Be Your Own Boss—People Weren't Made that Way.

This brings up an interesting concept. When you think how God designed man, you realize man is never "big" enough to be his own boss. He is either under God's authority or Satan's tyranny. We are either servants of God or slaves of Satan.

That reality surely runs counter to present philosophy that claims, "I am the master of my fate, I am the captain of my soul" (*Invictus,* by William Henley). A recent *Women's Day* article encouraged this concept by urging parents to pick up a baby every time it cried. This only taught the child at an early age that it was in charge of its life and circumstances! A belief that could only be shattered as the child grew.

John Bunyan in his story *The Holy War* did an excellent job of portraying the temptation of Satan to Mansoul to be the "captain of his fate," and the tragic results that followed. If you don't have the book, I would suggest obtaining a child's version to read to your children. Or, if your children enjoy tapes, Ethel Barrett has a tape of the story put out by Gospel Light Publications (Ventura, California 93006). My children loved it.

● Obedience Is More Important than Giving Presents.

We all love presents from our children—bouquets held up by chubby fists and kisses from smiling faces. When you hug those little cherubs and thank them for their gifts, you can tell them their obedience is just like a present, and you enjoy it every time they obey you.

● Obedience to God Gives Us Real Freedom.

As every mature Christian has learned, real freedom comes when we obey God. We are freed from the bondage of bad attitudes, enslaving habits, stress-producing resentments, and angry spirits.

ACTIVITIES AND THOUGHTS

This section is designed a bit differently than the other chapters. Since obedience covers the whole gamut of daily activities, the focus will be on handling specific problems typical of different ages.

One to Two Years Old

Babies are held when they hurt, fed when they are hungry, and given a pacifier in-between. Their attention span is so short that when they reach for a cup of coffee, we can give them something else and they are satisfied.

But toward the end of that first year things begin to change. (If we could include sound effects, drums should roll and cymbals crash at this point!) Now the difficult part of parenting begins. The problem is that we aren't sure how much children really understand. (Most of the time it is much more than we give them credit for!)

I watched a sixteen-month-old youngster in the church nursery the other Sunday. He picked up a good-sized, hard, plastic chicken and threw it across the room. His mother gave him a little speech about it not being nice to throw toys. He picked up another toy and, looking right at her, threw it as hard as he could.

Successfully teaching your child obedience may be as simple as correcting your child one more time than he disobeys.

He seemed to be saying, "OK, Mom. Let's see what you are going to do now. Are you really going to make me mind?" This little guy had more perseverance than his mother. It wasn't until he threw a toy that hit another child in the head that she jumped up and reinforced her words.

Two minutes later he was checking out the situation again. *Whish* went another toy across the room. And since he didn't hit anyone this time, his mother ignored him.

If his mother thought it was all right for him to throw toys as long as he didn't hit anyone, she should have said so. But, of course, at his age he had no control of his aim. So either throwing toys was fine or it was not fine. The mother needed to be clear and definite in her instructions—and in her discipline.

The earliest instructions we give toddlers are to protect life and property, so let's "dare to discipline." When your son or daughter has been told "No," and then, looking right at you, deliberately continues a forbidden activity, it is time to reinforce your words with consistent discipline.

The more self-willed your child is, the more crucial it is for you to begin training for obedience early. You can save yourself years of struggle and discouragement that way.

Another problem faced by parents of toddlers is what to do with the knickknacks around the house. I have heard a few parents claim they didn't have to put a thing away when their children were little. They just told them "No," and that was that! That must be wonderful, but it doesn't solve the problem for the rest of us!

Since this is a time of training, and training has mishaps, don't train with irreplaceable treasures. Put these objects out of reach. Then place a few less valuable, preferably unbreakable, objects within your toddler's reach. This is how children learn about the world around them.

Since he will have to learn to leave objects alone in other people's homes, practice with one or two fairly indestructible "pretties" on your coffee table. A practice session may involve an hour when you take your youngster on a tour of the living room and tell him, "Yes, yes, yes, no, yes, yes" as you go over the objects in the room. Then stick with the project until the one "No" object in sight is left alone. This may be especially helpful just before you go to visit Great Aunt Sue who lives amidst her cut-glass table decorations and who, of course, never had any children!

I still remember the trepidation I experienced whenever I went out visiting with my young children. In one second I could spot five irresistible objects my youngest would be after. Before I could get the first safely rescued, he was on his way to the next enticing spot! Even today, I try to put breakable knickknacks up when I know toddlers are coming for a visit. It is as much for the parents' peace of mind as for the protection of property.

At this age it is important to distinguish between childish awkwardness and deliberate defiance. If your youngster accidentally knocks her juice off the high chair onto the freshly mopped floor, she does not deserve punishment. Those are just the hazards of life and kids. But if she didn't like the kind of juice you poured and threw the glass on the floor in anger, you have quite a different problem on your hands!

Two to Eleven Years Old

1. During these years, a request as simple as "Come here" can elicit such a variety of responses that it can be the prelude to a training session in obedience.

First, there are the children who invariably have some reason they can't do what you want—not just now! For my child who was like this, we instituted special "No Talking Back" days—days that he was not allowed to make excuses, ask for a longer time, or complain about instructions in any way. On the one hand he didn't think he complained about instructions very often, and on the other hand he thought he would pop if he couldn't talk back.

I do believe strongly in teaching my children to communicate their thoughts, though. A later chapter deals with teaching this important skill. But any child can become a grumbler and whiner if it is to his advantage.

Having a "No Talking Back" day periodically has been very helpful to my son. He began to hear himself for the first time. "You know," he said one day, "I really do talk back a lot, don't I?" (Ah! We were making progress!) It became a project he could pray about and work on.

Then, one day when I was fixing dinner, my son poked his head around the corner of the dining room and announced, "I really am going to try to stop talking back."

Perhaps beginning "No Talking Back" days would be helpful for you and your child. If you do this, plans need to be made a day ahead of time. First, make a list of four or five incidents when the child was asked to do something. For example, set the table, carry out the trash, or feed the dog. Write down what she said in reply. With children it is very important to have concrete examples of problem behavior. Blanket accusations like, "You always talk back!" or "You never mind me" aren't sufficient. And they usually aren't true! (Last time you called, "Come and get a popsickle!" everyone came, right?) Even a child can pick out the weak link in a logical train of thought. The words "always" and "never" are two words that are sure to undermine your credibility.

Next, have a quiet talk with your child at bedtime. Go over your list of examples of talking back. Explain that tomorrow will be a different kind of a day—a "No Talking Back" day—and the child is to do her best not to complain about instructions you have given or requests you've made. In this way you both have a fresh, new day to begin the project, and it can be like a challenging game to your child.

Ideally, once they have been properly trained children don't ever talk back. But realistically this is like any other area you work on, see improvement, then need to work on again. You may want to begin this practice with your children somewhere between the ages of four and eight, depending on their maturity.

Of course, we want to be reasonable with our children. Occasionally when I call them, one of my sons will reply, "Mom, I'm on the last chapter of my book. Can I come when I'm finished?" We all know how last chapters are! So at that point I decide if I need him immediately or if I can wait ten minutes. Don't become an unreasonable tyrant. That only inspires rebellion.

A second response to "Come here" is the perpetual "Why?" In fact, some youngsters seem to make this their response to everything! I told our boys I would be happy to tell them why if they had already decided to obey and were just curious about the activity. But if their "Why?" was a prelude to arguing, then it shouldn't be asked. So occasionally we had to stop and find out what kind of "Why?" we had.

One thing to note: some youngsters have learned to use the little phrase "You don't love me" to great advantage, especially when they are being disciplined or told to do something they don't want to do. But children need to know you love them enough to discipline them.

2. With children at this age, your instructions need to be clear and specific. And don't say things you don't mean. Do you know the first thing a commitment to obedience made me do? I quit talking so much! Knowing I must stop to see that my instructions are carried out, I give only the important ones instead of talking continuously.

3. Realize that as a parent you are training all the time, even when you don't mean to be. It only takes one or two times of ignoring disobedience (when you are talking on the phone or reading a book) for your children to learn they can disobey when you're distracted, or that they don't have to mind until you have

spoken twice, raised your voice, or called them by their middle name, or, worst of all, that you won't correct them unless they have made you angry.

It can't be said too often: Whatever else you do with your children as you train them, be consistent!

Twelve to Fifteen Years Old
I was surprised recently by the question, "Well, what do you do with a twelve-year-old who is bigger than

God did not design man to be his own master. A person is either a servant of God or a slave of Satan.

you? You can't spank him!" Actually, manhandling a child simply because you are bigger than he is is inappropriate at any age (and certainly unnecessary if you have consistently disciplined).

As our children matured, physical punishment was not administered unless they acknowledged the fact that it was deserved. I wouldn't say there was any delight in receiving it—but correction was accepted with the same tolerance as Great Aunt Jessica's smothering hugs and kisses at a family reunion.

At one stage we had a problem with our boys leaving their dresser drawers open, their clothes dangling out in a three-tiered cascade. After many reminders I finally promised, "If I come by and see your drawers open and clothes hanging out, I will give you one swat with the belt for each open drawer."

Sure enough, when I walked by the door several days later, the clothes cascade was back. But as the culprit lay over the bed awaiting his just desserts, his greatest concern usually was, "Are any of my brother's drawers open? Do any of them get a swat, too?"

These are the years when authority shifts slowly from external control (parents, teacher, etc.) to self-control, and obedience is replaced by deference and consideration. So be sure you are showing the kind of thoughtfulness to your children that you would like to receive from them. If you would like to know where they are going and when they will be back, be sure to give them the same information when you go somewhere. If no one is home and you must go out unexpectedly, leave a note—just as you would like your children to do.

By the time youngsters reach fifteen or sixteen, they either do what you ask out of respect and appreciation for the investment you have made in all dimensions of their lives, or they do whatever they can get away with.

Here are some things you can do to make this transition time easier:

1. If you think of physical discipline as withdrawals from a bank account, you can see the importance of words like: "You did a good job"; "I appreciate your trying"; "You were thoughtful"; and "I appreciate your obedience." These are your "bank deposits." Be tuned in to keeping a positive daily balance, with more "deposits" of praise than "withdrawals" of correction.

2. Reserve the right to change your mind. It is no disgrace to make a poor decision, but it is a shame if you can't admit it. Usually your children know if you have been hasty and unwise. Their respect for you only grows when you can admit you were wrong. But when you change rules because you realize they need to be changed, be sure to tell the children why you're doing it.

3. If it's possible, don't let your children leave a time of discipline angry. If they leave angry you may have failed to do one of two things: to communicate why they were being disciplined or to discipline them sufficiently.

One note: you may have a child who needs a little time to resolve feelings of anger. If this is the case, give your child the time she needs. Then, sometime before the end of the day, get together with her to talk over what happened and resolve anything that still needs to be resolved. Remember, anger is not bad, but letting it last into the next day is. (See Ephesians 4:26.)

4. Explain the result of disobedience as a statement of fact and not a threat. The punishment should be something your child cannot realistically resent and that you have no cause to feel guilty about administering.

5. Don't be like many parents who are oblivious to their children while they are young, then panic when they realize their child has suddenly become a teenager and is old enough to get into real trouble! Especially because such a teenager is hardly prepared to relinquish the control he has had for years to a "restriction-wielding" parent who suddenly has decided to start investing time and concern in him. Start making time, concern, and relationship deposits now, to ensure you will have a balance to cover the discipline withdrawals you undoubtedly will need to make later.

Chapter Four. Dependability: Doing What I Know I Should, So Others Can Count on Me

Nathan stood in the doorway ready for school, "Now don't forget, Mom," he reminded me. His class was holding a bake sale, and I had promised to bring the brownies by ten o'clock. He was afraid I would forget, so he brought out the heavy artillery: "I'm depending on you!"

We had worked on the character quality of dependability, so he understood the weight of the words, "I'm depending on you!" I was caught by surprise, for it had been a long time since anyone had said that to me. I think he was glad to have such grown-up words to use. They worked, too, causing the responsibility I had accepted to settle more heavily on my shoulders.

When we worked on the character quality of dependability, the boys made our bulletin board definition by cutting letters out of an old newspaper. Since most children love scissors, this can be a fun activity right at the beginning of the month. (Though it probably would be a good idea to limit the kids' cutting to newspapers!)

I once read a comment that said something to the effect that we are living on the perfume of an empty vase. In other words, dependability, honesty, and integrity once were blooms whose perfume pervaded our society. God's Word provided the moral and ethical roots and branches for the blooming of these values. Qualities such as dependability were appreciated and encouraged by all segments of our society. Then philosophers thought they could remove the plant, God's Word, and retain the fragrance of the blooms. As a result these values are now ignored or ridiculed. So, the only way our children are going to develop these qualities is if we parents take an active role in living and teaching them.

Dependability is an important quality for you to teach. And it is a quality that will be increasingly important as your child matures and finds friends, employers, and family depending on him.

SCRIPTURE

Here are Scriptures to use as you teach your children dependability:

"Even a child is known by his doings, whether his work be pure, and whether it be right" (Proverbs 20:11, KJV).

"A good name is to be chosen rather than great riches" (Proverbs 22:1).

"As smoke to the eyes, so is the sluggard to those who send him" (Proverbs 10:26).

"He who is faithful in what is least is faithful also in much" (Luke 16:10).

As God unfolds truth in the pages of Scripture, he focuses the spotlight on many "big" people: prophets, priests, and kings. I like this first verse from Proverbs 20 because it highlights the importance of even the smallest child's actions.

One day when our youngest son was about seven he asked, "We have to be good because Daddy is Dr. Brown, right?" Many youngsters grow up with this misdirected focus for good conduct. Help your children

"I'm depending on you" could be just the challenge your child needs to strive to do his best.

realize they are establishing their own reputations and that is why they should be careful what they do.

To illustrate this, consider taking a trip to the pet store or neighborhood garage sale for visual aids. Buy a fish bowl, a couple of fish, and a few aquarium plants. Then let your children set the aquarium up. They will enjoy watching the fish, and you can point out interesting things in the behavior of the fish. For example, some fish hide in the plants, while others are curious and come to see anything that gets close to the side of the aquarium. There are even very aggressive fish that keep all other fish away from the territory they claim.

Your children will quickly pick up that they can learn about fish by watching them. Use this to help them see that that is how people learn about us: they see what we do and soon learn whether or not we are dependable.

(One note: If you and the children weary of cleaning up the fish bowl and the spilled fish food, have your own garage sale or donate the whole set-up to your local pet store. When our hamsters surprised us with sixteen babies, the pet store in town was kind enough to take the little ones off our hands!)

Consider the second verse, Proverbs 22:1. There are several interesting Bible characters whose lives illustrate dependability. Share their stories with your children at bedtime this month.

Abraham is one of these fascinating people. Even God, who knows everything about everyone, believed he could depend on Abraham. In Genesis 18:19 he declares, "For I know him [Abraham] . . . that he may command his children and his household after him, that they keep the way of the Lord." I can't think of a greater compliment than having God testify to a man's dependability.

It is good to use the Old Testament characters to encourage our children. Especially because God is faithful to record his people's failures as well as their successes. We make a mistake if we do not share the record of these failures with our children as they are growing up. What better way to help them learn that a successful, dependable man knows how to deal with both success *and* failure.

An example of this is recorded in Genesis 10:12-20. Here we see that earlier in Abraham's life he and his people traveled to Egypt during a famine in Canaan. As Abraham neared the country, he became afraid the Egyptians would kill him to marry his beautiful wife, Sarah. So he asked her to tell Pharaoh that she was his sister. It's true that Sarah was Abraham's half-sister, but she was also his wife. Abraham should have told the whole truth and trusted God for their safety; instead he told less than the truth and disgraced his name and God's name. God used Pharaoh to rebuke Abraham. Pharaoh was so angry that he told Abraham to leave the country. When he returned to Canaan, Abraham built an altar (Genesis 13:4) and asked God to forgive him.

This story can teach us an important lesson about what to do if we have not been dependable: we are to ask forgiveness of those we have failed, including God.

Job is another man who stands tall in the pages of Scripture. I don't suppose we often think of God as being proud of us, but he was proud of Job. He even wanted Satan to notice how dependable Job was, so in

Job 1:8 he asked, "Have you considered my servant Job, that there is none like him on the earth, a blameless and upright man, one who fears God and shuns evil?"

Satan took that as a challenge, and tried every trick he could to make Job disappoint God. But Job came through the tests with flying colors! What a wonderful goal for your child, to strive after being a dependable person, someone of whom God can be proud.

To illustrate the third Scripture verse (Proverbs 10:26), plan a family barbecue one day this month

The initial development of dependability will depend on your verbal reinforcement of the concept.

(weather permitting, of course). While you are barbecuing, call the children out to the grill and let them sprinkle seasoning on the meat or turn a couple of hamburgers over. When the smoke begins to bother their eyes (the wind is always more than cooperative when we use the grill), ask if they know what the Bible says about smoke getting in their eyes.

If they don't know, send them for a Bible to look up Proverbs 10:26. When they have read the verse, explain that a "sluggard" is a lazy person, someone who is not dependable, who does not complete tasks he has been sent to do. Then after supper have them draw a picture of your family barbecuing, illustrating the problem with smoke and including this Scripture.

This object lesson can show your children how important it is for them to be dependable. They won't want to be "smoke" in your eyes, or in the eyes of teachers and friends who send them on errands. This principle will most likely come to their minds many times in the future as they help barbecue.

Finally, in light of the last Scripture verse, begin encouraging your child to be dependable from age two onward. It is important for them to realize that dependability doesn't start at eighteen or twenty with big jobs. Rather, it is built when the smallest tasks—such as picking up toys, putting laundry away, feeding the dog, or emptying the trash—are completed consistently.

SLOGANS

Here are three slogans you can use as you teach your children about dependability:

- The Greatest Ability Is *Depend*ability.

Not every child has the ability to win a spelling bee or hit a home run, but dependability is a wonderful ability every child can develop. However, since few awards are presented for dependability, it will be up to you to establish its importance.

It may be that you are working on this character quality at a time when your child needs a real boost to his self-esteem. Report card time or Awards Day can be very disheartening for children of average academic ability, especially if they do their best yet never receive recognition.

If you feel your child needs special encouragement, work especially hard on this character quality, then plan an awards dinner at the end of the month. At the table present your daughter with a half dozen roses (or carnations, or daisies) and a card thanking her for her dependability. Or, give your son a trophy with his name, the date, and the words "Most Dependable Son" engraved on it.

- You Can Count on Me!

Every child knows what it is like to have a friend promise to come over, but never show up. If disappointments like this occur during the month, you can use them as opportunities to reinforce the importance of dependability.

- I Am a Boy/Girl of My Word.

If your child promised to play with a neighbor child but cannot go, let her telephone to say, "I'm sorry, but I can't come to play." Since letting younger children use the telephone is usually reserved for special times, this adds a grown-up aura to dependability and helps establish consideration of others. You will be one of those who benefit from such consideration in the years to come.

ACTIVITIES
Two to Seven Years Old

The measure of a man is not whether he fails, but what he does after he fails.

When you are sitting folding clothes, give your three-year-old a stack of washcloths with instructions to put them in the bathroom on the vanity top. Youngsters at this age are as proud of helping as if you had given them the crown jewels to put away.

Those little feet can save you many steps if you let them. God gave kids such an abundance of energy, I'm sure all of it wasn't supposed to be used festooning the sink, tub, and commode with half a roll of toilet paper; turning the dog's dishes over; or spilling a pitcher of Kool-Aid. Children's "unhelpful" activities are always with us and are so easy to complain about. But we can depend on our children to do a multitude of useful tasks if we take the time to corral them into helping.

When your child brings baby's bottle, or lets you know that brother is preparing for a swan dive from the back of the couch, praise him for his helpfulness. Saying, "I knew I could count on you" or "I'm glad you are dependable" will begin the process of developing this character quality. Believe me, the development of any character quality depends largely on your reinforcement.

Recently, we worked hard covering a muddy section of our church preschool playground with mulch. Among the half dozen workers was a little four-year-old who struggled with baskets of mulch that were almost as big as he. As the hours ticked by the other children grew weary of helping and wandered off, but Robbie stuck it out, carrying load after load. I was glad to hear an adult helper compliment him on his dependability: "My, Robbie, you sure are a dependable, hard worker!" His little face just beamed. And I noticed that after lunch he was one of the few children (or adults) who went back to work again.

Here are some tasks for young children to do. But you need to take the time to check that the jobs were carried out before you are able to praise your children's dependability!

1. Ask your child to fold a stack of washcloths or handkerchiefs from the laundry several times a week. The older the child, the more complicated pieces he can fold.

2. Give your child the responsibility of putting away what he folded.

3. Let your child call and apologize if he makes commitments he cannot keep.

4. Let assignments like "Take the paper to Daddy" be opportunities for your husband or the father-figure in your child's life to add encouragement for the child's dependability. (Be sure your husband is clued in ahead of time, so he knows to praise your child at the appropriate time.)

5. Assign your child a task to be done after an activity is finished. For example, ask her to put her glass and plate on the sink after she has finished eating.

Often, remembering to do something at a later time is the essence of dependability. Although small children have short memories, it is amazing how they remember half-given promises, made at thoughtless moments. If little David can forget you promised him a cookie or ice cream after lunch, then you can be sympathetic when he forgets to put his dishes on the drainboard!

Eight to Fifteen Years Old

Emphasis on time-related dependability should be the focus at this age. Many adult obligations—getting to work, turning in work projects, or even being ready to go to town with friends—require meeting deadlines. Now is the time to train your children for this kind of dependability.

1. When your child goes somewhere—to the library, for example—give her a specific time to return. If she doesn't have a watch, she can check with the librarian so she is sure to return on time. There are

When honor rolls are forgotten and the flowers of the homecoming queen have faded, dependability will remain a sterling quality.

many other opportunities, such as ending play time with friends, that require keeping track of time. It is sad we live in such a busy world—but as long as we do, let's use our involvements to learn dependability.

2. Homemade charts with chores listed on them are good reminders to budding dependable people. Let your child make the chart himself, and the two of you decide which daily and weekly tasks to list. Anything from brushing teeth to washing the car can be included.

I even find it helpful to let my teenage boys write out their own Saturday lists. They seem to feel a greater sense of responsibility for their chores when they write them out. Once we've struggled through who has to clean the bathroom this week, they can pretty well take it from there!

3. Give your child a weekly allowance dependent on how well she remembers to do her chores. If waiting until Saturday to get an allowance seems too remote for your child, you might want to try a different tactic. Give your youngster a stack of dimes or quarters at the beginning of the week. Then check her chart

daily to see that the necessary tasks have been completed. She gets to keep any coins she doesn't forfeit by forgetting to brush her teeth or to complete some other important task.

CAUTIONS

It would be unfair not to mention that there are children who struggle with a "personal disorganization" handicap, who seem to have a short-term memory disability. A child like this may go to the store with all his Christmas money in his wallet, only to lay the wallet down somewhere in the toy department. Or he won't be able to tell you what he did with the tool you just saw in his hand. Not only has he no idea where he put it, he isn't even sure he touched it!

To the normal parent, such a child seems unbelievable. But when you stop to think about it, we all know their counterparts in the adult world. These are the people who can never find their glasses or remember where they put their car keys.

It is easy to tolerate physical handicaps because we can see them. We aren't upset with a crippled child who can't win a race. Yet we also need to accept memory or other handicaps with patience, and be willing to encourage our children if they struggle with such a problem.

Chapter Five. Gratitude: *Appreciation of What Is Done for Me; Acceptance of What I Cannot Change*

Joni Eareckson Tada has been a great blessing to many because of her triumph over tragedy. Through her life we see that gratitude has little to do with circumstances, but everything to do with our reaction to and acceptance of them. In her book, *A Step Further,* Joni shares her realization that many people are just as tempted to give in to self-pity over the little inconveniences of life as she is over the major trials she faces. Unfortunately, many adults and children struggle with the "Why me?" syndrome over problems that fade into insignificance when put in a proper perspective.

My son experienced this recently. He sat dejectedly on his bed the other day nursing a cold. He wanted answers to some perplexing questions: "Why did I have to get a cold? Why does everything bad always happen to me?"

Running the risk of becoming a "Job's Comforter," I countered, "Would you rather have measles? No? Well, then, how about mumps? Would malaria be more exciting?"

Although he did not appreciate my questions, I had an important point that I wanted to communicate. Many times we don't get the answers we are looking for because we have the wrong focus or ask the wrong questions. For Joni, the focus eventually shifted from "Why me, Lord?" to "I trust you, Lord. In your time, let me see what you are doing."

For the Christian, gratitude can be a comforting reality in any circumstance. We can know God is in charge and nothing can come into our lives unless he permits it. As you teach your children about gratitude this month, here are three important things you should help them realize:

1. God is working out his purpose in their lives at all times, if they are obeying and trusting him;

2. There is evil and sickness in this world because of sin, and innocent people will suffer as long as we have physical bodies and Satan controls the lives of men; and

3. God will not allow any trial or temptation to come into their lives that he cannot give them grace to overcome if they depend on him—and he will bring good out of evil.

The two greatest hindrances to gratitude for children and adults seem to be circumstances and possessions. We question our circumstances because of what is or is not happening. And we are not thankful for what we have because of what we lack.

Whether your children develop into grateful teenagers and adults in spite of losses or unfortunate circumstances is in part up to you and how you help them handle their problems.

SCRIPTURE

Gratitude is a character quality that has a lot to do with our thoughts and attitudes. Because of this, the Scriptures this month center on our thoughts and how they affect us:

"A merry heart makes a cheerful countenance, But by sorrow of the heart, the spirit is broken" (Proverbs 15:13).

"For as [a man] thinks in his heart, so is he" (Proverbs 23:7).

Gratitude has little to do with circumstances, but everything to do with how we react to them.

"The eye is not satisfied with seeing, nor the ear filled with hearing" (Ecclesiastes 1:8).

The last Scripture adds a new dimension to the kaleidoscope of life. Children need to learn that just as their eyes and ears are always open to more sights and sounds, the human heart is always fascinated by something new and different. Many people think they will be happy and grateful if just one more desire is fulfilled. However, gratefulness is the fruit of contentment—and we don't find contentment by adding to our wants. Rather, contentment comes from subtracting from our desires.

Just sharing this truth with your children can help them change their thinking and discover that, like a kaleidoscope, the pieces in life's puzzle can be put together in different, interesting ways.

The second Scripture, "For as [a man] thinks in his heart, so is he," can be given a slightly different emphasis for children. For example, "Whatever a boy or girl thinks is what he or she is and will become," may be easier to understand.

If your youngsters are going to develop a grateful focus in life, they need to learn to use realistic thinking to balance or counter the negative thoughts Satan is busy putting into their minds. God tells us in 2 Corinthians 10:3-5 that in handling the problems of life, we must bring every thought into captivity, into obedience to Christ. Taking something captive, especially a thought, requires effort. It is part of the spiritual warfare we need to learn.

The questions our children ask are a clue to the kinds of thoughts they are thinking. Listen to them carefully; their thoughts may need redirection or an alternate focus. For example, can you think of positive responses for the negative thoughts behind these typically childish questions:

1. "Why did it rain today? God knew we wanted to go to the park!"
2. "Why did my toy car have to break just when I wanted to play with it?"
3. "Why does Sara always get everything she wants, and I never do?"
4. "Why do I always have to do all the work around here?"
5. "Why did my puppy get run over when I loved it so much?"

These are just a few of the great philosophical questions dads and moms are asked daily. Sometimes the answers aren't as important as just being there to share the disappointment or pain—but other times, strong, positive answers are needed.

Here are some possible responses to help you deal with these and similar situations.

1. "Do you realize that God has little children everywhere who want to go to the park to play? Some wanted to go to the park yesterday, and some want to go to the park tomorrow. But he also has trees and flowers that need a drink. In fact, they will die if they don't get enough rain! I know you are disappointed that we can't go to the park today, but we will try to go tomorrow or next week.

"Instead of being sad for yourself, try to be glad for the trees and flowers outside. They are clapping their leaves and thanking God for the rain! Besides, we can use the time we would have spent at the park to do something kind for someone else. Let's call Aunt Jane and you can tell her you missed her at church Sunday. Or, if you want, you can color a picture for Daddy."

Remind your child that whatever we do, we have a choice to make: we can accept the grace God can give us to be happy in spite of disappointments, or we can choose to be grumbling and unhappy.

2. "I'm sorry your toy is broken, but it was plastic and not very sturdy. We will try to repair it and it may last a little longer, but next time let's choose a sturdier toy. And you can be thankful you had your car to play with this whole month."

*T*he circumstances of life can make us better or bitter; the choice is ours.

3. "Sara doesn't get everything she wants. None of us do. There are lots of things we want but we can't have for one reason or another. Sometimes, even when we do get what we want, we have to wait for a long time to get it. So you see, we all go through the same thing. But you know what? I bet it would be much more fun to be happy for Sara than to grumble and complain. Then, when you get something you want, she can be happy for you!"

4. One response to this typical childhood question can be both fun and educational. After a tirade of, "Why do I have to clear the table? I always do all the work around here! Why can't my brother do it?" from one of our sons, I made a pair of construction-paper sunglasses, using a pair of my own to outline the frame. I stapled arms to the front piece and taped lenses made from colored cellophane in place.

The next time a barrage of grumbling started, I was ready! I got out my little creation and had my persecuted child put them on.

"Hey, what are these for?" my son wanted to know. "Everything looks yellow! Did you make them? Can I have them?"

"Why does everything look yellow?" I asked.

"Oh, because of this yellow stuff," he said pointing to the cellophane.

"When you take off the glasses, do things still look yellow?"

He removed the glasses. "No."

"Is everything really yellow?"

"No, I guess not."

"But when you have the glasses on you would think so, wouldn't you?"

"Yes."

"Well," I explained, "those cellophane lenses are like self-pitying thoughts. They make you feel you're being picked on. They don't let you honestly compare the work you do to the work of others. There is a lot to do around our home, you know: laundry, cooking supper, washing dishes, mowing lawns, washing cars, and a lot more. You don't do half of it, let alone all of it, now do you?"

"Well no," he said hesitantly, "but . . ."

"Have you ever seen a picture or a drawing of a little boy with an angel sitting on one shoulder and an imp on the other, both whispering in his ears?"

"Yes."

"Well, you can be sure it's the imp who whispers self-pitying thoughts and not the angel. How about if we work on learning who is coloring the thoughts in your mind so you don't listen to the imp and think you are mistreated!"

A final response to this question might be this thought-provoking quote from Alexander Pope's *Essay on Criticism*. Using the glasses as a visual aid may be helpful in getting the point of the quote across to your child:

All 'Tis Infected That the Infected Spy, as All 'Tis Yellow to the Jaundiced Eye.

5. The last question is more difficult, and certainly one that needs an answer. Here are some other thoughts you can share with your child at the appropriate time: "You loved Skipper, didn't you? I did, too, and I am sad with you. You tried to teach her to stay in the yard like I told you, but she was little and didn't want to mind. Let's try to be thankful for the time (week, month, year) you had her. You have all the happy memories of your fun together. Those memory-pictures and feelings are something you will always have, and you can be grateful for them. If you will let him, God will comfort your heart in your sadness."

Gratefulness doesn't come by adding to the sum of our wants, but by subtracting from the balance of our desires.

Whether it is a pet that dies or a family member, children eventually cope with the difficult question of death and loss. Both children and adults find gratitude easy in the happy times, but quite a struggle in times of sorrow and perplexity.

Part of the reason we struggle with this is that we misunderstand Scriptures such as Romans 8:28. Here we are told, "All things work together for good to them that love God." Unfortunately, we often confuse worldly good with true good. The greatest good for anyone is their spiritual good. It is living close to God, learning to really trust him and accept his workings in our lives. Joni shares in her writings that now she is able to thank God for her accident because of the spiritual growth and blessings she has gained. She is sure that because of her handicaps she is closer to God than she would have been otherwise.

We see through the story of Job that Satan is behind many tragedies. Yet we are promised in 1 Corinthians 10:13 that no trial or temptation will come our way without God making a way for us to escape. Once again, what we escape is spiritual damage—and the way we escape is by trusting God and accepting his grace and comfort. He can and often does protect us from pain. And someday he will take us to a place where there is no sorrow or death.

Through your own confidence and trust in God you may wish to share these truths with your children. Perplexing circumstances either make us better or bitter. Let's help our children choose, like Job, to trust God and become better.

SLOGANS

You can use the following three slogans as you teach your children about gratitude:

- Happy Thoughts Make Happy Faces.
- Let's Have an Attitude Check.
- Dear God, Please Guide and Guard My Desires.

Since it is especially important to develop gratitude in the area of our possessions, this last slogan can be incorporated into mealtime or evening prayers. Desires have a way of spontaneously generating from something as innocent as a catalog. Too often these desires have an amazing way of transforming themselves into needs. When this happens with your child, help him learn to ask God to guide and guard his desires.

I remember three-year-old Philip's first foray into the world of "wants." He sat with a Sears Wish Book on his knees, turning the pages, looking at everything intently. Then, "I want that" he said, his little finger pressed on a tricycle.

As my boys grew I felt it was important for them to understand that catalog browsing, like window shopping, too often just generates wants. Now when the boys get out a catalog, they comment with a grin, "I'm going to see if I can generate some wants!"

It will take a while to convince your children, but it is important for them to be told over and over again that they can never acquire enough "things" to make them happy. It doesn't matter how rich they are or how much they own. Real happiness comes only from contentment within—and contentment within comes only from a relationship with Christ.

Here is a practical exercise you can do to impress this concept on your child's mind. If your child commonly "has to" have a new or different toy every week (or even every month), greet his next toy request with a short discussion about the last toy he thought he absolutely had to have. (Keep track of that wingless airplane or broken motorcycle, so you know where it ended up.) Ask if he remembers standing in the toy section of the local department store wanting that toy with all his heart. Point out that he hasn't played with it for a week or two (if that's the case).

The point of the talk is not to scold him; a fascination with something new is a basic part of human nature. Simply try to help him see that what he wanted so badly two weeks ago now lays forgotten—and what he wants today won't matter nearly so much a week from now.

The "Guide and Guard" slogan/prayer is even useful for parents, since "wants" don't diminish as you grow up—they just get bigger and more expensive! This has become one of my frequent prayers. It has helped decrease my desires and increase my gratitude.

ACTIVITIES
Two to Seven Years Old

1. You can start developing sunny, grateful children from the cradle up by letting smiles be the passport to affection and hugs, instead of tears, whines, or tugs on your clothes.

During college I met a family with grown children whose oldest daughter was an unhappy, self-pitying person. Their other adult children were happy, pleasant people.

They shared with me some insight they had gained from rearing their children. When their first child was small, she had whined and grumbled constantly, and they had spent a lot of time trying to soothe and comfort her. When their second child was born, the parents agreed that from six months on he would only be picked up when he was pleasant. They began each morning by taking him out of his crib only after he had smiled.

Encouragement like "Let's be a happy boy!" or "Daddy wants a smile!" took only a short time to transform him from a baby who cried to get his way to one who smiled and cooed to be held. They attributed the happy, pleasant dispositions of their younger children in part to this difference in early training.

2. The simple process of teaching a two-year-old "please" and "thank you" begins the child's expression of gratefulness. So, don't bypass teaching these simple courtesies. Likewise, be sure to thank your children when they deserve it, for they are learning how to act by your example.

3. Make table grace and bedtime prayers creative times of expressing gratefulness. For this month dispense with the memorized prayers of, "God is great" and "Now I lay me down to sleep," and let each of your children make up his own prayer. You will probably enjoy this as much as your children! I still have those amusing transcripts I jotted down of four-year-old Nathan's eloquent prayers thanking God for "kids, corn, and queen-sized beds" (whose queen-size bed I don't know, for we never had one!)

If bedtime comes and your children can't think of a thing they are grateful for, have them make a list similar to the one below. Several different times during the following day, ask them what they have enjoyed doing or what they are thankful for. Then have them write down these things.

Today I Am Grateful For:

FLUFFY CLOUDS + SUNSHINE

MY BABY SISTER

POPSICLES WHEN I'M HOT

5. When your children exhibit a self-pitying mindset, deal with it. The thought patterns this mindset produces do not put situations in proper perspective.

As knowledge of human genetics grows there is increasing evidence that personality traits, like physical characteristics, are molded by heredity. Some youngsters come into this world with a natural tendency toward thought patterns that produce pouting and self-pity.

I first became aware of this tendency toward self-pity in one of my boys when he was not yet three.

G *ratitude cannot come from a dissatisfied heart, any more than a smile can be forced on an angry countenance.*

Grandma and Grandpa were visiting and had only been there a few days when this little fellow announced, "I don't like Grandpa!"

It took a bit of questioning, but I finally discovered the cause of this sudden aversion. "Grandpa bumped my head!" he declared.

It seems that upon return from an evening outing he had pretended to fall asleep on Grandpa's lap in the back seat of the car. He was a good actor, even at this age, and thought being carried into his bed was much more exciting than walking on his own two feet! So Grandpa, unable to awaken his charge, struggled to get out of the car with his limp burden in his arms. In the process he inadvertently bumped the child's head on the car door. There was no outcry or tears—that would have ruined the act, I guess—but resentment began to grow in my son's childish heart. There was no appreciation for the effort Grandpa had made to carry him to bed. In fact, all Grandpa got for his efforts was being black-listed! This incident alerted me to the challenge I had before me of developing a grateful attitude in a heart bent toward self-pity.

If this tendency is present in your child, you need to be aware of it. Such a child needs extra help making evaluations of circumstances that are in line with reality. If this tendency is left unchecked, it produces an immature adult who is easily offended. He or she cannot get along with anyone for very long, because eventually friends say or do something that offends them.

As hard as it may be to believe, you can point out unreasonable thoughts, even to a five- or six-year-old. In the car door incident just described, I ran through a series of questions like this:

"Did Grandpa ever bump your head before? When he held you on his lap yesterday, or played with you last night, did he bump your head? Then Grandpa didn't hurt you on purpose, did he? You stepped on my toes yesterday, but I said it was OK when you said you were sorry. You see, sometimes you hurt people by accident, too. If you stop to think about it, you know Grandpa didn't hurt you on purpose. Your attitude of self-pity even kept you from being thankful that Grandpa carried you to bed last night. Carrying someone to bed is hard work! How would you like to try to carry him to bed?!"

As my son grew older I had to deal with his self-pitying tendency in other ways. One day, when he was about eight, we were having guests for dinner and I had set his place at the drainboard because I didn't have room at the table. I knew he didn't like to have to sit at the drainboard, but I was still surprised to notice, about the time we reached dessert, that he had not eaten one thing.

I called him out of the room and asked what was wrong. With folded arms and a sullen frown he said, "You didn't give me a fork, so I didn't ask for anything from the table!"

I could hardly believe it! He set the table often and certainly knew where the forks were kept. But he chose to sit the meal out with nothing to eat because of the gross injustice of a forgotten fork.

In spite of my apologies, his resentment continued through the evening. After the guests left we had a talk, but I got nowhere. He seemed convinced that I had forgotten his fork on purpose. Finally frustrated with getting nowhere by using logic, I tried nonsense: "Well, I suppose I thought, 'My son is going to sit here and I don't want him to have any of this good food I have fixed. What shall I do? I know what to do! I won't give him a fork! Then he will have to go hungry!'"

By the time I finished talking, the absurdity of the whole thing began to dawn on him. He came to me later and said, "I'm sorry, Mom, for acting that way about the fork. Now I can see how silly it was to think like that!"

6. Another way to deal with a pouting spirit is to have a child stand in front of a mirror and look at the

G ratitude increases when we understand the effort it takes to perform an act of kindness.

face she is making. Let her see that her face is a mirror of her heart, and that angry, resentful thoughts make unpleasant faces. Both of you can face the mirror and talk about the problem until she can smile at herself.

Eight to Fifteen Years Old

1. Read books to your children about people who had strong faith in God and developed grateful spirits in spite of great difficulties.

The life of George Washington Carver, for example, is sobering and inspiring, as are the stories of Joni Eareckson Tada, John Bunyan, Helen Keller, and the Bible characters Daniel and Joseph.

2. For older children have supper be a place of sharing. Go around the table and let everyone express something they are grateful for that day.

3. To a significant extent, gratitude stems from understanding the effort it takes someone else to do a kindness for us. Be sure your children share in the work at home or they will not be able to appreciate what you do.

I heard a mother of grown children wearily complain, "I have worked my fingers to the bone for my children and all they do is take, take, take, with never a thank-you or an offer to help."

However, her children's perspective was a bit different: "Anytime we tried to help Mom, she'd say, 'No, I can do it faster than you can,' or she would find fault with what we did. So we just let her do the work!"

4. See that your youngsters write "thank you" notes for gifts and kindnesses done for them. Depending on their age, they may color a picture to include with the note, or send a snapshot.

5. Include your children in kindnesses that you do. If you make a casserole for a sick friend, let your child take it to the door when you deliver it. She will get to share in the person's gratitude and learn the joy of giving.

Chapter Six. Responsibility:
Telling Myself What to Do and Accepting the Results of My Actions and Decisions

"Don't look in my room, Mom!" Nathan called down the hall.

"Why not?" I wanted to know. Such requests always stimulate my curiosity.

"Oh, you'll see in a few minutes," was the mysterious reply. "But don't look until I tell you!"

It wasn't Christmas time and no birthdays were coming up, so I wasn't sure what to expect. Soon eight-year-old Nathan revealed his surprise: he had straightened up his dresser drawers.

"I did it all by myself," he bragged. "You didn't even have to tell me to!" Any dad or mom who has opened a child's drawers between the periodic cleanings, will appreciate, as I did, his accomplishment! When children are small it seems you will be telling them what to do forever. It is so encouraging when they finally begin telling themselves to do a few things!

If your children are small, just work with the first part of the definition for responsibility: "Telling myself what to do." For your older children, the concept of accepting responsibility for actions and decisions needs to be included as well.

Responsibility, like dependability or perseverance, is important in so many aspects of life that there are many ways to teach it. You may want to begin by choosing a special area where one of your children needs help. For example, if one of the children is often late for school or always the last one out the door when you're going somewhere, punctuality would be a good place to start.

However, since even a child is amazingly adept at denying his faults, improvement can't begin until he realizes he has a problem. You can pass that hurdle by discussing the situation—perhaps pointing out how many tardies were on the last report card and how often the family is sitting in the car waiting for the child. Then you can begin working toward more responsible behavior.

Sometimes children (and adults!) are late because they haven't really learned how much time is needed to perform daily tasks. If getting to school on time is a real problem, let your child begin his project by guessing how long it takes to get up and make the bed; how much time passes after leaving the bedroom until breakfast is over; and how many minutes it takes to brush his teeth, comb his hair, or get dressed. Then he can compare how long he thought it would take with how long it actually takes.

Consider making a chart and recording the morning schedule for several days. This will give your child something concrete to work with. I am sure comparing hypothetical times to actual times will be an eye-opener! Then the chart can serve as a basis for setting up a reasonable schedule that will get the child to school on time.

The second aspect of this month's character quality, "accepting responsibility for actions and decisions," isn't one of our society's strong points. So it will be up to you to instill this attitude in your children.

I received my first lesson in teaching this aspect of responsibility while I was still a college student. It happened in a rather interesting way, through our church outreach program.

The small church I attended did not actually have a bus for its "bus route." Instead, several college students picked up children with their cars. A friend and I had picked up Karin, a little six-year-old girl, for Sunday school for about eight weeks.

One Sunday I went to the door, and when Karin's mother answered my knock she took one look at me and turned to call her daughter. "Karin has something to tell you," was all she said.

"I don't want to go to Sunday school any more," Karin announced when she got to the door.

Then her mother went on to explain, "Karin made the decision to start going to Sunday school, so I told her she had to tell you herself now that she doesn't want to go to church anymore."

Later we learned a child in her class had been unkind to her, and that was why she didn't want to come. It was a shame there were problems in the Sunday school class. And it was unfortunate that her mother didn't take Karin to church herself. But her mother did do something very important: she taught a six-year-old to accept responsibility for her own decisions.

Sometimes having children accept responsibility for their decisions and actions is hard on the parents. We discovered this when we traveled with our boys.

One summer several years ago we were in Missouri staying with friends after a youth camp. They were an older couple with grown children and a living room full of fancy table decorations. I was in the kitchen helping prepare the evening meal when I noticed the boys poking their heads around the door, beckoning to me silently.

They had been in the living room, and I wish I could say they had been sitting like little cherubs reading books. Unfortunately, that was not the case! The pillows on the couch and chairs had attracted their attention and, you guessed it, they had been throwing them at each other. Of course, the inevitable had happened—something was broken! Philip, who had thrown the offending pillow, stood looking stricken.

As I inspected the ceramic dove with a now-broken wing, Philip screwed his eleven-year-old courage. He knew what he had to do. With a sinking heart he marched out into the kitchen and announced, "Mrs. Ferguson, I'm sorry, I broke your dove in the living room!" (Fortunately, it wasn't a family heirloom and it had been broken and mended before.)

I was tempted, as I'm sure you've been, to run interference for my son, to go myself and explain about the accident to our hostess. But let me give you a word of advice: don't do it! Your child will live through the trauma of accepting responsibility for his actions, and I can assure you he will remember the experience far longer than all the words of caution you give in the future!

However, you cannot expect your children to shoulder responsibility out in the big wide world if they don't get some practice at home. When they leave Dad's tools out in the grass for a week, do they acknowledge their forgetfulness? Can they own up to being the barber when the dog shows up looking like someone tried to give her a "buzz?" Stress the importance of responsibility for actions where it will have the most impact: at home!

SCRIPTURE
There are several Scriptures that have the same all-encompassing scope as the concept of responsibility. One of them is found in the Old Testament, and one in the New Testament:

"Whatever your hand finds to do, do it with your might" (Ecclesiastes 9:10).

"Whatever you do, do all to the glory of God" (1 Corinthians 10:31).

Another Scripture that embodies the inner commitment involved in being responsible is:

"I will pay my vows" (Psalms 22:25).

The value of being responsible or faithful is illustrated by the question asked in this verse: "A faithful man who can find?" (Proverbs 20:6).

SLOGANS

Use these three slogans to help you teach your children about responsibility:
- I Will Tell Myself to Do What I Should.
- I Will Accept Responsibility for My Actions.
- Privilege Brings Responsibility.

If you enjoy being creative, try making mobiles out of your slogans this month. The first slogan can be done with the child's picture above the word "I" and an empty toothpaste carton in the center.

The mobile can be made more specific by replacing "to do what I should" with "to brush my teeth," or any other task your child does. Wire clothes hangers cut with metal-cutters can be used to make the cross bars, and the words of the slogan written on construction paper can be hung with thread or fishing line. Once you get the mobile balanced, a spot of white glue will hold the thread and cross bars in place.

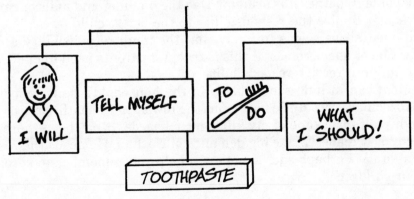

Consider the third slogan. Children love privileges, but they need to learn that responsibility goes along with privilege. If you allow your children to go to a friend's house, let them know they are responsible for conducting themselves properly. When they go out with friends, make it clear ahead of time that continued privilege hinges on whether they get home on time. This short slogan, "Privilege Brings Responsibility," ought to be repeated daily during this month. And you must do your part to see that privilege is tied to responsibility.

ACTIVITIES

A recent study of successful men and women identified one common denominator in their lives: they all were given a great deal of responsibility at an early age. Also, a significant percentage of them were either oldest children or children who were four to five years apart from other siblings.

When you stop to think about it, the oldest child usually is called on when a helping hand is needed around the house. Second and third children are "denied" these privileges because the older child is considered more capable. Whether it is bringing Dad the hammer and nails or carrying a dish to the table for Mom, it's just easier to give the responsibility to the oldest child.

The study mentioned above seems to imply that the more responsibility a child is given, the more responsible an adult he or she becomes. If this is true, we parents need to make a conscientious effort to see that all of our children receive responsibility.

Both Dad and Mom can include the children in the household's daily responsibilities. Let different children bring the broom, carry out the trash, put the towels in the bathroom, or bring Daddy the paper.

I have a note to myself inside one of my kitchen cupboards. It has been there for years as a reminder about my second child. It reads: "Make big demands of Nathan. He needs the responsibility and to know you believe he can do it!" Perhaps such a note will help you remember to spread responsibilities more equally among your children.

Two to Seven Years Old

For children this age, developing responsibility involves teaching what to do and how to do it. Children cannot tell themselves to do a task if they do not know how to do it (or even that it needs to be done). It is only after you have worked with your children many times—for example, showing them how to arrange dresser drawers by putting underclothes in one drawer, play clothes in another—that they can surprise you by doing the task themselves.

Letting your children live with the consequences of their actions prepares them for adulthood.

At times, of course, children will try to take on a task beyond their abilities. An attempt to surprise you with a cake may turn the kitchen into a battleground, with batter here and dirty bowls everywhere. Try to stifle your shriek and concentrate on the fact that your child showed initiative and started a big job all on her own! You should be impressed! She had perseverance too, for hopefully the cake (or a reasonable facsimile thereof) is in the oven. Now you can lend a helping hand with the clean-up campaign.

Recently I asked Nathan to trim the hedge in front of the house. He did a good job on that, then decided to square up the palm trees along the walk as well. When I returned from the grocery store the palm trees were decimated! I did my best to concentrate on his initiative, self-image, perseverance, etc., and asked quietly about the palm trees.

"Oh," he said. "Dad didn't like the fronds over the walk—anyway the ends of the fronds will grow out again."

We concluded the episode with a short botany lesson on the difference between the growth patterns of a hibiscus hedge and a palm tree!

Here are some suggested activities for children two to seven years old. Have them:

1. Make their own beds each morning. (Be sure you take time periodically to teach and reteach how it is done.)

2. Feed a pet daily.

3. Carry their plates and silverware to the sink after each meal.

4. Perform a household chore, such as carrying out the trash, daily.

Chore charts, with stars pasted in boxes or squares colored in after chores are completed, serve as an external reminder to children. Let them make up their own chart if they are old enough, and occasionally give them a two- or three-day stretch when they are responsible for checking the chart and seeing that it is filled in.

To reward your children's responsible behavior, have them cut out a crown and cover it with tinfoil. This can be kept on top of the refrigerator, and brought down to let your child be "Miss Responsibility" or "Mr. Responsibility" for a few minutes each day when they remember to do their chores.

For our family, brushing teeth was an opportunity for learning. We seemed to manage the tooth brushing pretty well, but invariably the toothpaste would end up on the floor without a cap. Of course each boy was sure the other was the culprit!

Finally I had a stroke of genius and I purchased two tubes of toothpaste. I printed the boys' names on paper in large letters, then used cellophane tape to protect the names from water and taped them to the tubes. Now everyone knew who was responsible for which toothpaste tube!

5. Brush teeth each night before bed.

6. Accept responsibility by paying their own library fines when books they checked out are overdue.

7. Learn how to make decisions and how to accept responsibility for them.

It's only normal that you make all the decisions for your children when they are tiny. As they mature, though, you need to let them make different types of decisions. It may be no more than how their hair is combed, what play clothes they will wear, or which shoes to wear on a special occasion. If your children tend to make inappropriate choices, let them choose from several items you select.

Of course, one of the biggest clothing decisions (and struggles) we face is the perpetual question of whether a sweater or jacket is going to be worn. Some self-willed youngsters need to be given the choice of wearing a jacket or going without occasionally. But this should be done with the understanding that if going without a jacket results in a cold, and a cold means missing a party the child is looking forward to, then that is the price she will pay.

Of course, I'm not talking about letting a child out in a snowstorm wearing just a T-shirt. But when the need is debatable, let your child decide part of the time. The most immature adults are those who have never learned to accept the consequences of choices they make. The sniffles may be the least costly price your child will pay for an unwise decision—and it can help them appreciate you as their counselor and adviser.

Eight to Fifteen Years Old
The degree of responsibility appropriate at different ages can be best understood by illustrating three ways of giving instructions for a single task:

1. "I want you to mow the lawn today. Start at three o'clock and stay at the job until it is finished."
2. "I want you to mow the lawn today. Be sure it is done before supper."
3. "I expect you to keep the back yard up, by mowing it once a week."

Let's look at the first instructions. Who, what, and when are spelled out for the younger worker. He has no decisions to make.

The second instructions are given in such a way that the responsibility for planning when to mow the lawn has been shifted to the child. He has several questions to ask himself. They include: "What time do we usually have supper? How long will it take me to mow the lawn? When should I start to be sure I finish before supper? Should I start now and be done early, or wait until the last minute?"

In the last set of instructions, the older worker is given the privilege of fitting the job into his schedule himself. No one is going to remind him. But with this privilege goes the responsibility of planning so the task is completed as assigned.

From these examples you can see that the tasks are not necessarily going to be different during these older years, but the discipline and decision-making will shift to the child's shoulders. The younger the child, the more prompts and external reminders will be needed. With an older child the "Post-a-note" reminders, chore charts, and nightly reviews of obligations can be fewer and further between.

Here are some specific activities to try:

1. Have your children increasingly assume responsibility for personal hygiene. When your children were three and four years old, bedtime probably was a marathon. You supervised filling the bathtub so it didn't overflow. You had to play Sherlock Holmes to find the toothbrushes hidden under the drainboard clutter. You probably even had to put the right amount of toothpaste on the toothbrush and struggle through two or three sets of teeth and dripping chins.

As your children grow, turn these responsibilities over to their increasingly capable little hands. They know how to squeeze a toothpaste tube—let's just hope they can confine the paste to the toothbrush and refrain from decorating the sink, their shoes, and the rug! If they do make a mess, you can supervise from the doorway as they accept responsibility for their actions and clean things up!

2. See that your child accepts more and more responsibility for homework assignments.

Some youngsters can't wait to be given homework in school. They want to do it just like big brother or sister. Others are overwhelmed with the prospect of any assignment they must complete out of the teacher's sight.

Tell your children completion of homework is important to you. Then help them in this responsibility by buying an inexpensive Day-Timer or planning calendar. This will lend the glow of maturity to the work. Explain to your children that they can help themselves not to miss assignments by rechecking their Day-

Timer and their books before they leave the classroom. That way they will arrive home with all the textbooks they need for the evening's homework.

Have your children tell you about weekly and long-term assignments so you can help them as they assume responsibility for science fair projects and book reports. School is a child's "job" for twelve years, and while getting "A's" isn't necessarily crucial, developing responsibility is.

A family in our congregation had a little fellow who had a serious problem with personal forgetfulness

*L*etting your children make choices
can help them see your value as a counselor.

and disorganization. This had caused the child and his parents real trouble since second grade. Papers worked on in class were only half done, or papers were finished and never handed in. The teacher sent notes home to Dad and Mom, but they never received them. The child assured his folks everything was fine and dandy at school, then lost or trashed papers he had been given to complete.

By fifth grade the school teachers were exasperated with the parents, and the parents felt they weren't getting any help or input from the teachers. After talking to my husband several times, and trying everything they could think of, the parents finally considered finding a Christian counselor to see if their son had an underlying problem that they were missing.

In the meantime, the church family began to pray for this particular need and the parents planned special times of fasting and prayer. And the Lord helped miraculously! In a few weeks the teacher called home saying, "I don't know what has happened to Justin, but he is doing so much better!"

His lackadaisical attitude toward his school work improved week by week, and before the year was out he made the honor roll! At the end of the year he received the award for "Most Improved Student." When his mother asked him what in the world made the difference, his explanation was, "God has helped me!"

Though this situation didn't require it, some cases will call for counseling. Justin's parents were thankful their problem with irresponsibility was worked out without it, but they would have been willing to seek help in that area had it been needed. Also, as you work on these character qualities, remember you have a heavenly Father who wants to help you and your children. Learn to depend on him, for there are no unimportant problems with a God who has numbered the very hairs of our heads!

Caution

Perhaps a word of caution about homework is in order. If you are unhappy with the amount of homework your child receives, talk to the teacher about it. Whatever you do, don't grumble about assignments in front of your child! You will reap a harvest of grumbles for years to come for the few seeds of grumbling you thoughtlessly sow.

Chapter Seven. Stewardship: *Handling Money Wisely*

Remember the Bible story of the wise man and the foolish man in Matthew 7? The wise man built his house on a rock, and the rain descended, and the floods came, and the winds blew, and beat on that house—and it stood firm. But the foolish man built his house on the sand. . . .

My husband and I sat in a house built on sand recently, listening to a shower of tears pour down, and the winds of financial adversity howl. A newly-saved young couple was trying to come to grips with financial collapse. They had a house full of new furniture, two new cars, five or six credit cards run to the limit, a fluctuating mortgage payment, a new baby—and job problems!

None of us would wish this trauma on our children. But it is an all-too-common situation for many young couples. How sad, when it often could be avoided if parents would teach their children how to handle money while they are young.

For the first eighteen years of life, children learn how to earn a living. They are taught addition, subtraction, and those brain twisters that ask, "If Tom has two apples, and Sue has three apples, and Tim gives Tom half his apples. . . ." Still, children seem to get little practical preparation for handling the million or so dollars they will earn during their working years.

Fortunately, this is changing in the Christian community. Books, tapes, and seminars on biblical principles of finance are available. I have been especially thankful for the workbooks designed for children. *God's Guide Through the Money Jungle* by Larry Burkett (Christian Financial Concepts, Dahlonge, GA 30533) is one my boys enjoyed. It is so interestingly illustrated that you will need to be sure your children study the written material and don't just look at the pictures! This kind of workbook would be a valuable supplement to the concepts you want to teach your children regarding stewardship.

Also, keep in mind the biblical guidelines for training from Deuteronomy 6 which we discussed in Chapter 3: "These words which I command thee this day shall be in thine heart: And thou shalt teach them diligently unto thine children" (KJV). In light of this Scripture, it is safe to assume that financial responsibility needs to be part of your life-style before you can teach it to your children. If this is an area of your life that needs Christian discipline, let me encourage you to begin working on it this month so you can adequately train your children.

Bible scholars tell us that over half of Christ's parables deal with proper use of money, and much of Proverbs gives wisdom about finances. So this certainly is something God is concerned about.

When my husband and I married, we were very poor. Both of us attended graduate school full-time for five years, and we lived on a small monthly stipend from an academic scholarship. Still, we consider our early frugal years a blessing because we learned to trust God and to meet our needs creatively. (While a "solar-powered" clothesline stretched between two trees is less convenient than an electric clothes dryer, it is also much cheaper!)

At that time the government classified our income as below the poverty level. But we always paid our

Children cannot learn to handle money if they do not have some way to earn it.

tithe, had something to eat, were never late with a bill, and managed to save a little money each month.

Because we got along so well on our limited income, I used to wonder what other better-off people did with all their money. The Lord has blessed us financially since that time, and I have found out! But those early years of training still help us forego many small self-indulgences in order to afford major purchases and travel.

It also is reassuring to know we can go anywhere in the world that God wants us to go and do whatever he directs, because he will care for us and we can get by on very little.

Although neither my husband nor I had any accounting training, we always recorded our earnings each month. We wrote down each penny we spent and what we spent it on, then balanced our records against the checkbook. It is very interesting now to get out the little record books of those early years and look through them with our boys.

(If you want to help your children be financially responsible, or wish you had a better handle on your own finances, perhaps the procedures we share with our church couples will bring order to your financial chaos. That information is included at the end of the chapter.)

SCRIPTURE

There is certainly a wealth of scriptural wisdom on finances from which to choose.

"Honor the Lord with your possessions, and with the firstfruits of all your increase" (Proverbs 3:9).

"'Bring all the tithes into the storehouse, that there may be food in My house, and prove Me now in this,' says the Lord of hosts; 'If I will not open for you the windows of heaven and pour out for you such blessing that there will not be room enough to receive it'" (Malachi 3:10).

"The borrower is servant to the lender" (Proverbs 22:7).

"He who gives to the poor will not lack, but he who hides his eyes will have many curses" (Proverbs 28:27).

The first verse mentions "firstfruits." That's an interesting word, isn't it? You might encourage your children to put it in big bold letters when they write up the Scriptures this month. This word teaches that their giving is not to be taken from what is left over after a trip to the store. Rather, it is to be set aside when money is first received.

The second verse is rather long, but if your four- or five-year-old can memorize all the books of the Bible he probably can manage this as well. I have included it because children are masters at asking thought-provoking questions such as, "Why does God need my dime? Is he poor?" This verse is an excellent tool for answering this question and helping your child understand tithing.

The first reason for your children to tithe comes from the part of this verse that says, "that there may be food in my house." Your children need to know that God provides for his work on earth through their giving. Their dimes and dollars in the offering help buy the Sunday school papers and lesson booklets, pay for electricity and heat, and provide for missions and outreach.

The second reason for your children to tithe is that this provides God an opportunity to "prove" himself to us. By giving to God's work, we all acknowledge his role in providing for us and show our complete dependence on him. He is delighted when we accept the challenge to bring all the tithes into the storehouse, and trust in him to provide for us (which he does, even more abundantly than we can imagine).

You cannot teach what you do not know or give what you do not live.

Since children think in concrete terms, it is easy for them to remember that a tithe is ten percent of earnings. But spiritual freedom and blessing is missed if they do not understand why tithes and offerings are given. Plan time during family devotions this month to read the two Scriptures above and share these truths.

Also, share with your children your own experiences of God's financial provision. It will encourage them to watch for God's work in this area of their lives.

One of my important childhood memories centers around a time of God's provision. One Saturday morning my mother had gone shopping to pick up a few items at the dime store and then get the groceries. After an hour or so my father called us children in from the yard. He told us that mother had telephoned in tears. While she was shopping she had laid her purse down when paying for some socks, and someone had stolen it!

The police came and checked the area, but the purse and her grocery money were gone! With four children to feed on a teaching salary, the loss was a major one.

My father gathered us around the couch to pray. He thanked God for his provision for us and reminded him that we always honored him by tithing. Then we all prayed that somehow the purse would be returned if that was his will.

A short time later my mother drove up, and Dad went out to meet her. When he opened the passenger door, Mom's purse fell out onto the driveway. The money was still inside!

What a time of rejoicing we had!

The only explanation my mother could give was an incident that occurred as she drove away from the dime store. She noticed that the man driving in the lane next to her kept watching her. When they stopped at a traffic light, he sat staring at her. She was weeping and so turned away to avoid his gaze. Perhaps he had stolen the purse and God had convicted him. Possibly, in remorse, he dropped it in the open passenger window while her head was turned. Regardless of how God answered that prayer, it was a lesson in trust that I have never forgotten.

The third Scripture verse illustrates the reality of borrowing. It seems that even children who have never heard the word "borrow" still know how the practice works. I remember all those pleas of— "Mommy, Mommy, I don't have my dime. Will you buy me gum? I will give you my dime when we get home!" (One note: I have finally figured out how to actually receive my remuneration! Now I keep the gum, toy car, Popsicles, or whatever until the obligation is met!)

Borrowing can become quite a problem for some children, especially if they want to borrow on the strength of money they have not yet received. (I am sure you have heard the protests, "But I will get my allowance Saturday!") Here, as in other areas of childrearing, the challenge is mixing reasonableness, good sense, compassion, and principle in equal proportions. We encourage our children to get by as much as possible without borrowing. And we only lend to them when they already have the money needed to repay the loan. We are working to instill in them principles that they will need to apply to most of their purchases later in life.

Now, read the last verse again. A look at stewardship would not be complete without encouraging your children to think of money as a tool to benefit others. This Scripture gets this point across. It is a Scripture that took on special meaning for me when our family was privileged to spend six weeks in South Africa

Don't deny your children the privilege of learning some lessons from failure; it can be a very effective teacher.

several years ago. When we encountered a few beggars along the streets of Johannesburg, I noticed myself turning my eyes away. Later, when I came across this Scripture, I was convicted for my lack of Christian compassion.

SLOGANS

You probably have some visual aids around the house that will help in teaching stewardship. See if you can find that old piggy bank, then have the children ink a big dollar sign on a small spiral notebook that can serve as a record book of a growing savings account. Use these slogans to summarize financial responsibility:

- Saving Is Part of Stewardship.
- Giving Is Part of Stewardship.

- Record-keeping Is Part of Stewardship.
- Planning Is Part of Stewardship.

Here are the four foundation stones on which to build a firm financial policy: giving, saving, record-keeping, and planning. Each one will need to be worked on at different times throughout your children's growing-up years. But keep in mind that their personal maturity and ability to apply these principles will increase with time. So don't be discouraged if they make little progress the first time you work on these concepts.

ACTIVITIES

Two to Seven Years Old

It is amazing how early children begin developing ideas about money.

I remember my confusion when the boys at five or six years old kept insisting all I needed to do to solve my money problems was buy something. "Buy it, Mom," they urged with bright smiling faces. "You'll get change back!"

Change back? How was getting change back going to help me?

Finally it dawned on me that after observing a number of transactions where Mommy gave the clerk one bill (a five or ten dollar bill) and got several bills back (one dollar bills), they had decided people had more money after a purchase than before!

Children in these years begin appreciating the usefulness of money, too. When Philip came home from kindergarten after the first report cards were given out, he was all excited about the financial rewards his friends received for their grades. He had worked hard learning the alphabet and thought he should be rewarded, too!

Because he couldn't learn to manage money if he didn't have any, we agreed to a reward policy. We would give him one dollar for each "A" he earned in academics and five dollars for an "A" in conduct.

Somewhere along the line, as his knowledge of finances grew, he managed to have the reward policy expanded to include the heady sum of five dollars per "A" if he received straight "A's." With six grading periods per year and some fourteen possible grades each time, that became a formidable financial commitment. Fortunately he didn't hit the jackpot too often!

Part of the policy was that the first five dollars he earned each grading period went into a savings account. Just going to the bank to open a savings account was a big foray into the world of high finance for a five-year-old. There was an extra benefit, too: the quarterly reports sent on the account provided him the thrill of receiving personal mail!

Here are some suggestions for you to follow as you help your children learn to handle money wisely.

1. If it's at all possible, provide your children with a means of earning money through allowances or extra work—even if it's a very small amount.

2. Require them to tithe some of their money to God so that they learn about giving.

3. Buy them a small notebook and work with them recording their earnings, gifts, and expenditures.

4. Take them to open a savings account or buy a savings bond. Dad, this may be a special project you want to initiate. You may even want to have grandparents involved in this.

5. Help your children learn to accept financial responsibility when they incur expenses, such as paying their own library fines when books they checked out are overdue.

6. Teach your children discernment in evaluating the toys they buy. They will be able to apply the principles to important purchases later. You can see easily whether a car or doll is worth the money, so now is the time to teach your children to evaluate merchandise. When your children are ready to make a purchase, take time to talk to them about the strengths or weaknesses of several different kinds of the toys they are considering. Is the plastic or metal in the toys easily breakable or durable? Are the wheels going to fall off at the first bump? Is the doll's hair washable? Are the eyes securely in place?

After you have considered these things, you may veto the purchase if it seems it would be a poor choice. Or, if the cost is relatively small, you might let your children go ahead with an investment you think is unwise. They will learn far more about buying from one poor decision made on their own than from twenty good decisions you make for them. Just be certain you let them make their decisions in a context of love and acceptance. It will be much easier for them to acknowledge a mistake if you have not ridiculed their choices.

Eight to Fifteen Years Old
As I prepared to write this chapter I began to wonder how successful we had been in teaching financial responsibility to our boys. We've tried to teach so many things, sometimes I wonder how much of it really sticks in their minds after all!

To find out, I made a list of what we had shared with them. Then I asked the boys separately what they could remember about our talks on finances over the years. Between the two of them, I was pleasantly surprised with the results.

Here are the concepts the boys remembered and some ideas of how you can teach them to your children.
   • "I am only a manager and not an owner of the money I earn."
The concept of stewardship of money as opposed to ownership is a difficult one for children to grasp. From their earliest nursery days they protect what they want, warning playmates, "No! No! Mine! Mine!"

Our sense of possession and territorial protection seems to be part of our divinely designed human nature. God acknowledged and sanctioned it when he separated the Garden of Eden from the rest of his creation and gave it to the first two people to tend and guard.

But caring and keeping were to be administered under God's leadership. This part of our character, along with many other human traits, has been warped because of the Fall of man.

To help your children develop the concept of stewardship, you need to remind them throughout this month that health and strength are gifts from God. It is only because of these gifts that they have the ability to earn money. Also, help your children include God in their financial dreams by asking him to guide and guard their desires. Encourage them to pray about purchases they want to make. Pray together as a family before shopping trips, asking God to help you find needed items at reasonable prices.

- "The tithe should be paid first, then the rest can be used for savings or other things."

"Mommy, do you still go to heaven if you don't pay your tithe?" my son whispered urgently during a church service.

The offering was being taken and the usher had just stopped at our row. The plate was moving toward us. I knew Nathan hadn't brought any money with him, although he had some he could (and should) have given.

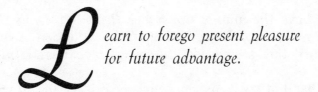

Learn to forego present pleasure for future advantage.

Actually he was very blasé about his money—except when it came to giving to God. He could be given a dollar one minute and lose it the next—no tears, no problem! But just let his dad suggest he give a dime in the offering and his fingers tightened around his money.

All these thoughts were racing through my mind as I checked on the progress of the plate. In panic I thought, "I've got three seconds. If I say 'Yes,' he'll feel absolved from giving to God for the rest of his life. If I say 'No,' well, I'm not about to damn my child at seven!"

I accepted the plate handed to me, turned to my son and whispered back, "We'll talk about it outside." I passed the plate on, then gently took my son's hand and we left the church. It didn't matter that my husband was the special speaker at the service, or that we were expected to be there. The most important business at that moment was that a child was suddenly ready to learn about God, money, and giving.

We found a quiet place on a bench outside and had a most profitable time discussing many of the ideas mentioned in the Scripture section of this chapter.

- "God expects me to plan carefully when I think about buying something so I get the best value for the money."

When the boys wanted to purchase a basketball or a bicycle, we took them to the library and showed them how to use *Consumer Reports* to find the best buy in their price range.

As they reached their teen years we included them in the research for items we needed, such as lawn mowers or cars. After all, someday soon they will be responsible for making these decisions in their own homes.

Your local library should have the annual *Consumer Reports Buying Guide,* which condenses the findings from their monthly magazines. It provides a quick evaluation of value per cost on hundreds of items we all purchase. If more details are needed, the reference to the monthly magazine is given and can be checked.

This may sound like a bother, but try it just once and see if it doesn't prove very helpful. You can plan the trip to the library on one of your family nights this month, and familiarize yourselves with this useful shopping tool. It will help your children (and you) protect themselves from the pressure of propaganda as they consider purchases.

- "I need to save money for emergencies."

Like the time Philip had to pay for his own new glasses after leaving them on top of the dog house for the second time in a month—he forgot the dog liked to eat them!

An allowance for chores, report-card earnings, and the occasional odd job for others should provide your children with a small but steady source of income in their early years. At first you will need to require them to save a portion of their earnings. Soon they will start saving on their own for vacation money or purchases they want to make.

- "Don't use credit cards unless you already have the money to pay for what you are buying and you pay the bill off the same month it comes in so there is no interest charged."

In this day of credit-card buying and easy loans, we want to protect our boys from the miseries of indebtedness. We have one major credit card we use to arrange plane fares or make major purchases by phone. But when solicitations for additional credit card applications arrive, or those marvelous letters come informing us that all we have to do is cash this $500.00 check and have money for whatever we want, I save them to use as object lessons with the boys. I want them to know how easy it is to fall into the trap of borrowing money with little concern of how it will be paid back. The boys get to tear up these checks and applications and throw them away—which I hope will prepare them to resist temptation in the years ahead.

- "Learn how to take care of the yard and car yourself, so you don't have to pay someone to do it."

Though it's probably easier for parents to do car maintenance by ourselves, we need to teach our teenage children—boys and girls—how to do practical chores, like change the oil. I'll admit it has its hazards! The first time our oldest changed the oil in my car, the transmission froze up—somehow he'd managed to drain the transmission fluid and oil in one operation! But with guidance from you, car maintenance learned at home will be like extra money added to a young couple's budget!

This also is true of other repairs. Recently someone tore the flag off our mailbox. The family's first reaction was, "Oh brother, now we have to buy a new mailbox." Instead, Nathan thought he could fix it. He took on the job of designing and installing a new flag using materials we already had at the house. It took several attempts and suggestions from different family members, but using scrap wood, red paint, and a screw and bolt we all saw what can be done to save money by attempting a bit of creative work.

- "You need to write down what you spend so you can keep track of your money."

You can spare your children tears and grief by beginning now to encourage them to keep written records of their earnings and spending. The records need not be elaborate and can be kept on notebook paper or in a spiral notebook. If the children are small and have a minimum income, the following simple accounting should be adequate:

Date	Previous Balance	Earnings	Spent/ Given	Comments	Present Balance
JUNE 10	$5.43	$1.00		WORK FOR DAD	$6.43
JUNE 14	6.43		.10	OFFERING	6.33
JUNE 19	6.33				

If they have a weekly income the format opposite will work.

Here is a summary of what you can do this month to help your older children develop stewardship:

1. Teach your children the difference between "owning" and "managing" their finances.
2. Encourage them to include God in their financial dreams by letting him guide and guard their desires.
3. Include giving to God's work as part of their stewardship plan.
4. Teach your children how to research purchases in *Consumer Report.*
5. Incorporate the ideas of saving and giving money as soon as your children have a consistent income.
6. Explain the use and abuse of borrowing and credit-card buying.
7. Encourage creative problem solving to conserve money.
8. Insist on record-keeping for all earnings and expenditures.
9. Teach financial responsibility by having your children pay for items they break or lose through repeated carelessness. (But please mix a liberal dose of mercy with training here.)

Date: Week June 10-16

Previous Week's Balance
(June 3-9) $100.00

Earnings

1. ALLOWANCE $5.00
2. LAWN JOB   8.00
3. IN FROM SAVINGS ACCT. FOR TENNIS RACQUET   30.00

Total $ 43.00

Expenses/Giving

1. CHURCH $1.30
2. GAS FOR MOWER   1.00
3. TENNIS RACQUET   30.00

Total $ 32.30

Savings

1. SAVED FOR VACATION $5.00
2.
3.

Total $ 5.00

Summary Week June 10-16

Previous Balance + Earnings $143.00

Expenses + Savings   37.30

Balance for Week of June 10-16   105.70

Summary of Savings Activity

1. Previous Balance $50.00

2. Savings used
   (1) USED FOR TENNIS RACQUET -30.00
   (2)

Running Balance $20.00

3. Money Saved
   (1) SAVED FOR VACATION   +5.00
   (2)

Final Savings Balance $25.00

Final Thoughts

I want to add a postscript to this chapter for parents who feel they need to set their own financial house in order, and so help their children avoid the pitfalls they themselves are in.

Invariably we find that couples in financial difficulty do not keep written records of how they spend their money. They excuse themselves by saying it is all written on the check stubs, but that is not sufficient. To get on your feet financially, you need to keep a written record of every penny you spend for a month.

While you are doing this, begin compiling a list of monthly expenses, overdue bills, family loans, and any unpaid bills. Then begin by working with the bills that are due monthly. These are divided by four to find out how much of each weekly paycheck must be allotted for each item, for example:

Rent—$400 ÷ 4 = $100
Electricity—$100 ÷ 4 = $25
Water—$16 ÷ 4 = $4
Car payment—$300 ÷ 4 = $75
Total = $204

Now you know that before you eat, drive the car or insure it, you must save $204 out of each week's paycheck to cover your basic expenses. The cost of groceries, gas, car insurance, and any other constant expense must be added together to give you an idea of the minimum weekly earnings needed to exist. If there are unpaid doctor bills or you owe friends money, include these in your monthly expenses as well. Even if you can pay only five dollars a month, your creditors will know you are trying and will respect the effort. This is especially important to maintain your testimony as a Christian. (At this point, extra working hours or a second part-time job may be in order!)

Once these parameters are established, your goal should be to save one-fourth of your month's living expenses each week, so that you will have the total amount needed when the bill is due. Work at this slowly until you are ready and waiting when each bill comes. If you discipline yourself in this way, you will discover what real financial freedom is, and your checking account will never be overdrawn.

After two or three months of working weekly on your finances, keeping strict account of things, you will begin to see some hope for the future! Then it is time to incorporate into your weekly savings plan those bills that come due every six or twelve months.

One especially positive note: every three months there is a fifth (or "extra") week in the month. If you have kept up, the money from this extra week will not have to be used for the monthly bills. This can give you an opportunity to get ahead a little, or to buy a needed pair of glasses, or whatever.

After about six months you should be ready to begin a systematic repayment plan on overdue bills. Please realize that all vacations and self-indulgent purchases must be put on hold while your obligations are being met.

When we begin working with a couple who are behind on the rent and don't have enough grocery money for the week, the very idea of saving money for bills not yet due seems impossible. But as they keep track of where their money is going, cut down on all unnecessary expenses, pay something every month on overdue bills, put God in charge of their finances (and show their trust in him by paying a tithe), they are amazed.

God blesses them and stretches what they make in an unbelievable way. And he keeps away the devourer—car breakdowns, doctor visits, washing machine repairs—just as he promised to do (Malachi 3:11). Remember, God made the Israelites' shoes last forty years on the desert sand and stones. And he is just as willing to help us if we will trust him!

Some of the most satisfying experiences of our ministry have been helping young couples, or even couples married twenty years, find financial freedom through biblical stewardship. We rejoice in their happy exclamations telling us, "Hey, things are going great financially! We can't believe it! We have our bills paid, and are even saving a little money!"

Such is God's wonderful (and workable) guidance and provision.

Chapter Eight. Discernment: *Recognizing and Choosing the Best*

Does it take harmony to have music? Is design important to art? Can good be distinguished from evil? Are some choices right and others wrong?

As a Christian parent, I'm sure you are concerned about the answers to all these questions, and you want to teach your children discernment in these areas. At one time it was not difficult to tell the difference between music and noise or art and graffiti. Now there is a blurring of what is considered lovely and ugly, sense and nonsense, good and bad.

Often parents realize too late that it takes more than church attendance and family devotions to integrate biblical discernment into the myriad value judgments young people make, and that parental modeling alone is not enough to transfer values from one generation to the next (as the desertion of traditional values in recent years shows). Values and discernment in decision making must be taught systematically.

To teach discernment to your children, you need to know two things: what values you believe are important and how you teach them to a child. Both of these things are important factors in keeping your children from adopting today's societal values.

As you begin this month, Dad and Mom, sit down together and decide what it will take for your children to have the best life possible. Is completion of high school important? Does musical accomplishment rate high on the list? Do you expect your children to dress in a neat and clean manner, or does it matter if they embrace whatever fad follows on the heels of the punk rock movement? Do you have strong feelings about politics, business ethics, financial success, or friendships? Use a paper and pencil as you talk, to keep a record of your ideas.

Discernment is needed in the whole gamut of human relationships, and you as parents must decide what you want to pass on to your children.

SCRIPTURE

Here are two powerful verses to use as you and your children study and discuss discernment:

"The wisdom of this world is foolishness with God" (1 Corinthians 3:19).

"Whatsoever things are . . . lovely and of good report . . . think on these things" (Philippians 4:8, KJV).

What is the basis for making value judgments, for recognizing and choosing the best? For the Christian, it is biblical principles. True discernment needs a moral foundation.

Although the Bible is primarily concerned with the revelation of God's redemptive love, it includes his ideas on everything from life goals to art, music, and literature. By pointing out the very best in all these areas, it helps establish a grid for separating the valuable from the worthless.

Unfortunately God's guidelines aren't the only ones on the market today. The world also has a grid of guidelines, and is very proud of its so-called wisdom. It is constantly bombarding us with the acceptability of its ideas and ideals, and with the absurdity of scriptural principles. Unfortunately, the more we listen to the world's rationalization and "wisdom," the more reasonable it seems, and the more difficult sound value judgments become.

Consider, for example, the present evaluation of homosexuality. The world has recently transformed it from a perversion to an "acceptable alternative life-style." How did this happen? By replacing God's guidelines with the world's evaluation!

The verse from 1 Corinthians 3 shows us God's commentary on the world's wisdom when it rejects biblical principles and substitutes its own: "The wisdom of this world is foolishness. . . ." This is a good Scripture for your children to learn as the foundation for developing discernment.

Let's take something that may be a little closer to home. What about art? Is "beauty in the eye of the beholder," or does God have guidelines for discernment in the aesthetic areas of life? Apparently God does have some standards for what is good, lovely, and acceptable, because he indicates in the second verse that all things are not equal. There are certain things we should be thinking about, and there are other things on which we should not waste our time and energy!

We can see God's standards for beauty in his creation: "Then God saw everything that he had made and indeed it was very good" (Genesis 1:31). From the most delicate seashell to the mightiest oak tree, God's handiwork was good. His art gallery gives us lessons in spatial dimensions, color mixing, symmetry, and proportions—the whole spectrum of art. Surely we can pass to our children an appreciation of the beauty he has shared—and an understanding of the fact that there *are* good, biblical standards to which we should adhere.

SLOGANS

Because discernment covers such a wide scope of life, there are many slogans that can be used. Here are a few:

- We Are His Ambassadors.
- His Standards Are My Guidelines.
- His World Has Harmony.

In light of the last slogan, consider how the Greeks discovered some of the mathematical principles underlying the beauty of God's creation and incorporated them into their art. They analyzed the proportions of the human body, laying the foundation for Renaissance artist Michelangelo's painting of the Sistine Chapel. They applied the "golden rectangle" from nature to architecture and built the Parthenon, a building admired for centuries for its beautiful proportions.

Even in the world of the microscope, order and organization reigns. From the complexity of a single cell to man "fearfully and wonderfully made," we see harmony in divine artistry. How wonderful it is that God has provided us in his Word with guidelines for discernment in evaluating everything, even art.

ACTIVITIES

Use the activities this month to help your children establish, strand by strand, a grid to use in evaluating all areas of life. I have presented activities for developing discernment in several different areas, including life goals, vocational or educational goals, standards of dress, toys and recreation, literature, and art and music appreciation.

Life Goals

I hope one of your goals is to rear children who love God and want to place him at the center of their lives. If it is, you can help your children to discern the difference between decisions that place him there and decisions that set him to one side.

One of the saddest things I have seen is parents who love God but are awed by worldly success. Their children pick up that admiration and often become doctors, lawyers, or successful businessmen and

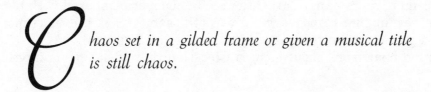

haos set in a gilded frame or given a musical title is still chaos.

women—yet they do not include God in their lives! If living for God is the most important thing in the world to you, be sure it is evident in what and whom you admire and in your words and actions.

Here are some activities you can do at home to help affirm the importance of God as the center of life.

Two to Seven Years Old

1. First and foremost, see that living for Jesus is the most important focus in your life. Then, during this month and periodically in the months to come, tell your children daily that serving Jesus is the best way to live. (Remember the admonition in Deuteronomy 6:6-7 to talk to your children. Here is another place you need to apply those instructions.)

2. Follow up with questions. Ask your children frequently, "What is the most important thing in life?" After a few promptings they should be able to quickly respond, "Serving Jesus!"

3. Read the Bible and Bible storybooks to your children daily. After all, the Bible is the foundation for Christian discernment. It certainly deserves ten or fifteen minutes each day.

4. Pray and work for an early commitment on your children's part to a personal relationship to Christ. God promises to give wisdom to those who ask him, and he will help you discern the best ways to accomplish this without pressuring or pushing your children.

5. Contrast career choices with a life commitment. My husband has shared with our boys many times one of the distinct memories from his childhood. As he grew up he went through the typical stages of wanting to be a policeman, a fireman, a carpenter, etc. Whenever he shared with his mom what he was going to be when he grew up, her response was always the same, "Son, it doesn't matter what you do in life, even if you are a garbage collector—as long as you are a Christian!"

Be sure your children hear more about being a Christian than about being anything else!

Eight to Fifteen Years Old

1. In the pre-teen years, you need to begin telling your children that living for God is the only intelligent way to live. Remember, the Bible says the man who ignores God in his life is a fool. The natural mind resents this evaluation, but it is true nonetheless.

An intelligent approach to any situation sees the end from the beginning, and considers long-term benefits. Christ warned that if a man gained the whole world and lost his soul, he would have lost everything. And there are no better long-term benefits than those God offers us through his Son, Jesus Christ!

2. Again, follow up with a question. Ask your children, "What is the only intelligent way to live?" Up to the beginning of their teen years, they can still benefit from question-and-answer times.

3. Help your children begin to add God's perspective on wealth and material success to their grid of discernment. These are the years when they want to know why, if serving God is so smart, your family isn't as rich as Mr. and Mrs. Uppercrust who live in the mansion on the hill. Let them know that God likes

to give material blessings to his children, but his primary concern is for our spiritual good. God knows how quickly the material things of this life pass away; he wants to give us lasting riches.

4. Include your children in prayer about major family decisions. Is the family thinking of moving? Is a job change under consideration? If your children know you pray about important decisions they too will learn to depend on God when they need discernment.

5. Let your children see you reading the Bible and praying. The sight of you on your knees praying will have more impact on them than a dozen bedtime prayers you help them say.

6. Help your children establish a personal time of Bible reading and prayer. Buy youth devotional material, Bible study workbooks, whatever they need to make Bible study interesting.

7. Point out to your children the heartache and tragedy that comes into the lives of people as a direct result of living without God. Did you read in the newspaper about a rich, famous person who committed suicide because he "had nothing to live for"? Consider sharing this with your children. It may help them keep worldly success in an eternal perspective.

Vocational or Educational Goals
Do you have vocational or educational goals for your children? Here are some special considerations to include in your thinking about this topic.

Two to Seven Years Old
1. Be sensitive to your children's God-given talents and abilities—God's guides to your children's lifework. There is little point in encouraging a child toward a career in music if she can't carry a tune! Ask your children what they would like to do. They may have interests they have never shared with anyone.

2. Give your children opportunities to explore their interests. Get books and films from the library that explain about different occupations so your children can learn about the opportunities available in today's world.

There are some jobs that are not really options for Christians, (i.e., if deceit is an intrinsic part of the occupation). If this is the case, you need to point this out to your children.

3. Don't try to live your life through your children or force them to become what you always wanted to be. Tell them they are free to be whatever God wants them to be.

Eight to Fifteen Years Old

1. As your children get older and their interests begin to crystallize, help them explore possible job opportunities. If your daughter thinks she wants to be a nurse, take her to visit a hospital or arrange a talk with a family friend who is in nursing. If your son is interested in carpentry, plan to spend one Saturday this month helping him work with simple plans for building a birdhouse. This is a good way for children to find out if they enjoy the work—or if they do not like it at all!

2. Help your children put career interests and socializing in focus. Many people have been frustrated all their lives because early marriage short-circuited the education they needed for the job they wanted. Early dating is unwise if post-high-school education is a necessity. Your children can develop discernment in this area by observing the lives of young people four or five years older than they are.

3. When your child is around fifteen years of age, you should spend an evening studying the newspaper with him. Let him figure out how much he will have to earn weekly to afford rent, car payments, clothing, food, medical care—the necessities of life. It will be a real eye-opener—one that will help him better evaluate whether his job interests coincide with his desired standard of living.

Dress Standards

A walk through the local mall is sufficient to show your children that people today look rumpled, faded, and torn. So far the nineties have been the "years of the sloppies."

One of the first things your children need to learn about clothes is that the way they dress affects several things: how others react to them, how they perform, and even how they think about themselves.

It is interesting that the first "wardrobe engineer" was a school teacher named John T. Molloy. In his book, *Dress for Success,* he tells about a study he did on the effect teachers' clothes had on students' attitudes, discipline, and learning in the classroom. In his first experiment he used two teachers who taught the same students in separate half-day sessions. One wore casual clothes—penny loafers, no suit coat, and a tie slightly open at the collar. The other wore traditional black laced shoes and a conservative

*C*lothing decisions should be based on knowledge, not ignorance.

suit and tie. Interestingly enough, the results of the study showed that students worked longer and harder for the teacher with the traditional, conservative look.

Since this initial research, Mr. Molloy has conducted hundreds of experiments on clothes, determining how they affect the people who wear them and how others react to what is worn. He has discovered that most of our reactions to clothes occur on a subconscious level. For example, if a man in faded jeans meets a neatly-dressed businessman on a narrow walkway, he steps aside to let the well-dressed man pass, often without even thinking about it.

Although Molloy's books (he has another book entitled *The Woman's Dress for Success Book*) are addressed primarily to business people, they enumerate principles that apply to all of us in different situations. I have made use of these principles in the classroom by dressing in a suit when I return tests to college students. I have less arguing and grumbling about the test scores that way!

I would not be so bold as to delineate a "Christian" pattern of dress, as Molloy does proper business attire. The point I wish to make is that our children need to know that how they dress affects how they feel about themselves and how other people respond to them. They should know that if they "dress up" they will get better service from sales people in a store. They will receive better treatment when they have to return merchandise if their appearance says, "I am important, I value myself!"

If your goal for your children is a standard of dress above the lowest common denominator, you are going to have to react to the sloppy and unkempt, and include your children in that emotional reaction. It is not enough to have dress standards for yourselves and then expect your children to automatically model them as they grow up. There are too many other "models" vying for their allegiance. Make your opinions and preferences, and the reasons for them, clear from a very early age.

Two to Seven Years Old

1. Choose a "dressed-up" standard you are comfortable with and want to see your children accept when they become teenagers. Make the guidelines specific, and begin teaching them by two years of age, if possible.

In keeping with our life-style of church work and college teaching, we set the following guidelines for our boys: Sunday morning—white shirt with top button buttoned, tie, dress pants, and dress shoes; Sunday night—dress shirt, dress pants, tie optional, and dress shoes; Wednesday night prayer meeting—casual shirt, jeans (but no holes!).

When we traveled in South Africa, we added another dimension to our knowledge of clothes: cultural appropriateness. After the boys wore jeans to an evening service, our hostess informed me that jeans were considered inappropriate at church and quite disrespectful to God. In fact, she said, even "sinners" wouldn't think of coming to church dressed like that!

Choose standards you are comfortable with and which fit your life-style. But be careful not to set them too low!

Of course it takes work to sell any set of standards to children. One of our boys hated a tie as early as four years old and declared he would never wear one when he grew up! But we insisted he wear one and bragged on him every time he dressed up. As the years went by his self-esteem was enhanced by a neat, clean appearance. By the time he was ten, he took great delight in dressing up, and even did so around the house!

If your girls complain about dress shoes, or the boys say a tie chokes them, buy a bigger size! One Father's Day, my husband preached on passing values and standards from fathers to sons and gave this very suggestion. Later, one of our parishioners told us he had gone out the very next week and bought three shirts for himself in a larger neck size. "No wonder I hated ties," he said. "I don't know why I stayed in tight, uncomfortable shirts for so long!"

2. Set specific standards for school dress. Young people who attend private schools with a dress code have an advantage here. Everyone in the school is required to "dress for success." There are several public schools in our area of Florida with voluntary attendance policies that require uniforms or have a rigid dress code. They find this contributes to fewer discipline problems and higher student performance.

It is especially important to establish a standard of school dress if you are home schooling. Consistency in school time and school dress will help develop a school mindset and spare you many problems. I encourage you to choose dresses for your girls, since you are trying to teach them to be ladies. Also, shoes should be a must for the home classroom. Play clothes can be put on later. Mom, you should take time to dress properly for the classroom setting, too!

Work with your children in establishing guidelines that balance excellence with appropriateness and fit in with standing alone. If you have worked consistently to establish dress standards while your children are little, by the time they start school you will be working together rather than against each other.

3. Use visual aids to contrast your standards with sloppy standards. Old Sears or Penney's catalogs are great to find the contrasts you need. Have children cut the pictures out and paste them on colored poster board. Have the children write evaluations above the pictures, "Neat," "Sloppy," "Good for Church," or "Right for School."

4. Give your children the task of looking through a catalog or newspaper (after Dad has a chance to see it!) and finding pictures of people they think exhibit different character qualities. Ask them who looks as though he will finish the job, be the most dependable, be trustworthy. (These are the kinds of studies Molloy did on clothing to find out how appearance affected potential employers or customers.) You will be surprised that even a young person will label people with certain appearances as dependable, trustworthy, careless, or irresponsible.

One note: realize your children will be making value judgments based on appearance, while God makes judgments based on the heart. It is a fact that in our society a dirty, torn, and faded look says something different about a person than does a neat and clean appearance. But help your children understand that a person's appearance does not determine his or her value to God. Yes, he wants us to look our best—but the most important factor is the state of that person's heart and his relationship with God. Remember, God accepts us just as we are.

Eight to Fifteen Years Old

1. Take time during one of your family nights to visit your local bookstores together and purchase John Molloy's book, *Dress for Success*. The younger your children are when you do this, the more opportunities you will have to use his principles of dress. The book is written in a very interesting manner, and the explanation of Molloy's different experiments will be fascinating even to most eight-year-olds.

2. Look through catalogs or magazines and have your children tell you which person looks like a bank teller, a bank manager, a construction worker, a college student, or a high-school drop-out. Doing this helps reveal subconscious evaluations.

3. As you establish your family's personal standard of dress, be sure to have a discussion on accepting people who have dress standards that differ from yours. I realized the need for such a discussion when our oldest was four. One Sunday when we were leaving church, Philip noticed a boy in a T-shirt coming out

the door. If a four-year-old can sputter, he did. He was so indignant he could hardly articulate words. "Imagine that!" he exclaimed, "Wearing an undershirt to church!"

From that point on we included acceptance of others as part of teaching about dress. By providing possible explanations for why people dress the way they do (they do not know any better, they cannot afford anything else, they like different kinds of clothes, etc.), you can teach your children to establish and hold dress standards you approve of without criticizing or rejecting other people.

Toys and Recreation
Two to Seven Years Old
You would think that something as innocent as children's toys wouldn't need much scrutiny. But if you and your spouse haven't been paying attention to what is on the toy store shelves lately, you need to begin checking so you can decide what is and is not acceptable in your home.

1. Choose toys consistent with the values and character qualities you are trying to teach. Before we had any children I can remember telling my husband, "If we have any little girls, they can have baby dolls to play with, not these leggy, busty movie star dolls I see."

There were several reasons I did not want these dolls for my children. First, the people they represented were not the kind of people I wanted my children to idolize. Such people all too often live life-styles that are anything but good and godly.

Then many of the items of apparel were not what I would want my children to wear when they were older. It made no sense to establish one set of values by my dress and life-style, yet permit daily interaction with something I would disapprove of for them personally. How could I expect my children to establish a set of values contrary to what was acceptable in their daily playtime?

Also, I did not want my girls to make outward beauty and perfection the model for femininity. I hoped to establish inner beauty and godliness as their ideals.

At that time I had never heard anyone express concern about little girls' dolls. Since then, however, I have been reassured to hear Dr. James Dobson react negatively to the impact these kinds of dolls have on young girls.

Yes, we do live in this world. However, you can choose things from the world that are consistent with your standards and ideals. You have a choice as to which toys you buy and what gifts you let the children keep.

2. Teach your children a biblical basis for evaluating toys themselves. This way, the values you are teaching them will become their own, not something you force on them.

Do this by stopping in the toy section of the local department store periodically on your trips to town. Pick up some of the menacing monsters with claws outstretched and blood dripping from their fangs. Many of these things are not just unsightly, they border on the demonic. Tell your children that they are ugly and that you will never have things like that in your home. From the time your children are three on, your reaction to the unsightly and bizarre will be key in molding their values. Remind your children that God says to make things that are lovely and of good report a part of our lives—not things that are monstrous or grotesque.

If you continue this practice monthly from the time your children are three or four, you will help them establish a solid grid for evaluation.

3. Use pictures from toy catalogs to contrast the lovely and the monstrous, the useful and the frivolous. Let the children cut these pictures out and tape them to construction paper, then talk about it around the supper table.

4. Be sure you spend twice as much time talking about those things that are lovely and acceptable as you spend pointing out the negative things. Like it or not, negative things have a stronger impact on our human minds. So be sure to make the good things of God your main emphasis when talking with your children.

Eight to Fifteen Years Old
The same activities and emphases need to be given to your youngsters during these years, so that when they begin personalizing their own rooms their posters, knickknacks, pictures, and decorations won't be nightmare material.

Literature
From the rarefied heights of poetry to the simplicity of Peter Cottontail, literature can be a delight. Unfortunately, not all that is written is pure or of a good report, so discernment is needed here, too.

Two to Seven Years Old
During these years you will be reading to your children. Your choice of material will help set the stage for their choices later.

I learned a lot from my first experience reading a major book to the boys. I had read the usual bushel of Golden Books over the years, but when Philip was five I thought we were ready for a real book. We were driving from Florida to California, so I chose the unabridged story of *Pinocchio* (I had never read it), and a child's version of *Pilgrim's Progress*. When we had finished the books, many miles down the road, my son's response was, "Mother, don't ever read *Pinocchio* to me again. They lie and cheat and are mean, but you can read me *Pilgrim's Progress*. I like that book!"

My college literature training had all been secular, so I wasn't quite prepared for his response. It was a valuable lesson that showed me the importance of discernment with literature. I realized the books available to my boys should be consistent with the other values and character qualities I was trying to teach them.

Here are some recommended books:

1. *Winnie the Pooh* by A.A. Milne
2. *The Tale of Peter Rabbit* by Beatrix Potter
3. *Play with Me* by Marie Ets
4. *What Do People Do All Day?* and other books by Richard Scarry
5. *Bambi* by T. Salten
6. *Just David* by Eleanor H. Porter
7. *Jungle Doctor* by Paul White
8. *Treasures in the Snow* and other titles by Patricia St. John
9. *Pilgrim's Progress* by John Bunyan
10. *Charlotte's Web* by E.B. White
11. *Billy and Blaze* by Russell Hoban
12. *Heidi* by Johanna Spyri
13. *Robinson Crusoe* by D. Defoe (the unabridged edition is wonderful to read to a child)
14. *The Lion, the Witch, and the Wardrobe* and the other Chronicles of Narnia by C.S. Lewis

An excellent resource book to have on hand is *Honey for a Child's Heart* by Gladys Hunt, which includes an annotated bibliography of books for children. Also, Hunt shares many good ideas about the use of books, types of books, and much more.

Eight to Fifteen Years Old
There are so many exciting, delightful stories and poems that will challenge your children to be their best. I hope you will encourage them to read. At the same time, you need to use biblical guidelines to evaluate the available literature and teach your children how to distinguish good reading from bad. Here are five steps to help you in this area.

1. Your children should be taught that anything suggestive or immoral is out. (See Ephesians 5:12.)
2. The literary heroes and heroines in your children's books should not contradict the values you are

teaching your children. A year or two ago I purchased a couple of children's detective books for the boys for Christmas. Before wrapping them I read through them. I was shocked to find the young detectives lying and expressing pride over having done so with a straight face!

In another instance, Philip had found a very interesting fantasy series at the library. In the middle of the third book there was a paragraph about the heroine having three children by different fathers, and their having been fostered out because she was too busy protecting the colony to care for them. Up to that point in the story there hadn't even been mention of boyfriends, let alone children! The very casualness of the reference was more eloquent in undermining morals and family values than pages of didactic dialogue would have been.

3. Read your children's books before they read them. I know that is a big order if your children are avid readers. Since we do not have a television, our boys read extensively. And my husband works hard to keep ahead of them when they bring home stacks of books from the library. Believe me, this is a necessary step. If you don't read your children's books, you won't have any idea what ungodly philosophies and standards they may be glorifying.

4. Include trips to used bookstores and garage sales as family-time outings. You can get books for your family library at a very reasonable price that way. And old books more often promote upright character qualities and traditional values.

I noticed recently that a new Nancy Drew series is going to replace this standard work for young girls. A remodeled heroine, complete with tight jeans, rock music blaring from her fast sports car, and looser morals is going to replace the church-going Nancy of years ago. So just because a book or book series was acceptable when you were a child doesn't mean it still is today.

5. Help your children develop a sensitivity to the occult in their grid of literary discernment. God's abhorrence of witchcraft and anything associated with Satan is mentioned over and over again in Scripture. You need to be aware that it is becoming a common topic in children's books (even the new Hardy Boys and Nancy Drew books), and warn your children about it.

The Arts
The arts play an encouraging and uplifting role in our lives, and Christians should have an "increasing sensitivity to beauty, and not a gradual blindness to ugliness" (Edith Schaeffer, *Hidden Art*, Tyndale House Publishers).

Man received his first lesson in art from a master artist, the Creator, who formed light from a bouquet of colors, then used the mist of a waterfall and the splendor of dewdrops to reveal his hidden rainbow. God dipped his paintbrush in this bouquet and clothed the grass of the fields with wildflowers. And his world testifies to his standard of what is good.

Because we are made in his image, we have a deep appreciation of beauty and a need to surround ourselves with it. Out of that need, art, architecture, sculpture, and music were born. Genesis records the birth of artistic creativity as far back as Adam's grandchildren. Some of them were workers in brass; others created musical instruments.

But somewhere along the line, worldly wisdom began telling us that disharmony was nice, and noise was music. Sadly many of us swallowed the lie. But when artistic expression captures and parades the confusion and hopelessness of degenerate man, we need to reject it. We must reaffirm beauty as typified by God's art gallery.

You can help your children increase their sensitivity and discernment of the arts a number of ways.

Two to Seven Years Old
1. Plan a "sunshine" spot in your child's room that she can decorate with the beautiful, delightful things she finds (i.e., a picture of a baby animal or a bouquet of dandelions from the lawn). As children look for different pretties for their "sunshine" spots, their eyes will be opened to the beauties of God's world.

2. Give an honored place in your home to special works of art your children create. The refrigerator door or a bulletin board can display their artistic attempts and encourage budding talent. I recall an elephant my brother whittled from a bar of soap that adorned the piano for years as I was growing up.

3. Point out artistry wherever you see it. The order and organization of a mist-bejeweled spiderweb helps establish the basic criteria for true art. And parents can enjoy such beauty anew when they see it through the sparkling eyes of a four-year-old.

Eight to Fifteen Years Old

1. As your children grow, expand their horizons of artistic appreciation by introducing them to architecture. There will be so many opportunities for your children's personal satisfaction when they actually

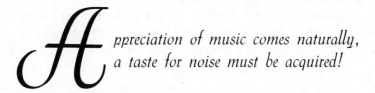

ppreciation of music comes naturally, a taste for noise must be acquired!

recognize a Tudor-style house, or a church built in classic Greek design with Doric columns.

If this is not an area in which you are knowledgeable, spend one family night studying architecture together in an encyclopedia. The next vacation, or even the next drive around town, will provide opportunities to test your new learning.

2. Share with your children a basic knowledge of colors, textures, and shapes. A sunset seen on a drive to church can provide a lesson in blending shades of a single color.

Your decorating at home provides material for teaching, too. Our boys learned an interesting lesson on the effect of color on visual perspective when I papered the end wall of a long narrow bathroom. The cupboard fronts were black formica, and the vanity top was white formica. I used a black wallpaper covered with a sprinkling of dainty pink roses. They were amazed when the combination and contrasts of colors made it seem the room had been shortened by several feet!

3. Continue your emphasis on order and harmony, as illustrated in creation, as the basis for art. It is said that bankers learn to detect counterfeit money by working hours and hours with the genuine article. As your children learn to appreciate the symmetry, proportion, balance, and harmony in God's world, they will gain an inner discernment and naturally reject the grotesque and hideous.

Music
The Greeks discovered order in music when they realized notes an octave apart were mathematical multiples or fractions of each other. The string that plays a "C" note, when divided in half and made to vibrate, produces the same sound an octave higher. Other notes which harmonized with the "C" sound can be made with the same string by using sections that are a third or fifth of the length.

Music is another area God designed to enrich our lives. But it too has potential to be used for good or ill.

Two to Seven Years Old
1. If you want your children to enjoy music rather than acquire a taste for noise, begin during these years to surround them with good religious, classical, and popular music. Your radio will help you in this project. It will also give you an opportunity to teach your children the sounds of different instruments—the trumpet, violin, French horn, etc.

2. Provide your children with piano or other instrument lessons if it is financially feasible. This is one of the best ways for them to learn the fundamentals of music.

3. Purchase several religious tapes with quiet, soothing music to put on when your children go to bed. This can be a wonderful opportunity to reinforce your values through music and turn your children's minds toward God as they go to sleep each night.

4. Let your children know your feelings about the noise that is passed off as music. Make your disapproval clear.

Eight to Fifteen Years Old

1. By this age, children need to start realizing the significance of the words that go along with music. When you are out in public and cannot avoid lewd lyrics, talk to your children about the lying, cheating, and immorality that is glamorized, and how much such things displease God.

2. Encourage your church to bring in seminar speakers who can explain why simply adding a label of "religious" to some kinds of music doesn't make it good or wholesome.

3. Read books that discuss the difference between music and noise as part of your family devotions.

4. Take your children with you to hear an occasional symphony concert if they are available in your city. And you might check with the local park around the Fourth of July to see if any patriotic band music will be played.

5. Consider limiting the home radios and stereos to a single, parentally-controlled central unit.

As a teenager I saw so many parents in conflict with their children about their music, I decided my children would not have a radio or stereo of their own. They would have access to the "community" equipment, but nothing in their bedrooms. We told the boys this from the time they were tiny, so it never became an issue. In fact, I have heard them brag to their friends about their lack, saying we cared too much about what they might hear to let them have a radio.

However, if you work diligently on teaching musical discernment your children should be able to have their own equipment by their late teens, without creating any problems.

Chapter Nine.
Communication:
Telling You My Thoughts and Listening to Yours

"What are you talking about?" Nathan asked, as he came into the living room where his father and I were talking. He had asked that question many times over the last few months. Often the topic of conversation was related to church counseling and was not for his little ears. So, time after time our response was, "You don't need to know this," or "This is not something you should hear."

Children are learning about communication all the time, and sometimes the conclusions they draw are not what we wish to convey. In this case, Nathan didn't like being left out of the conversation. So he decided that withholding information was synonymous with being grown-up.

Now, when you are four years old there aren't many people in your world to withhold information from. So Nathan decided to have secrets from us. Months went by and we didn't realize what was happening until he began responding to questions by saying, "No one needs to know what I think! I can have secrets, too!"

The situation reached a climax late one evening after a school Thanksgiving program that included a film about life in early America. On the five-minute drive home, Nathan began to sob. Expressions of concern produced a flood of tears, but no explanation of what was troubling him. This was not the first such episode, and we finally realized that if the communication barrier he was building didn't begin to crumble soon we would be in real trouble.

When we reached the house, the rest of the family went inside, and Nathan and I sat in the car in the dark, silent garage. At ten- to fifteen-minute intervals I asked, "Why are you feeling sad?" or "Did someone say something to make you feel bad tonight?" But most of the time I just sat with my arm around him comforting him, leaving the silence for him to fill.

Well over an hour passed before he suddenly burst into tears again and sobbed, "It was the Indian!"

At first I had no idea what he was talking about.

Then I remembered a short segment of the film we had just watched where an Indian was injured. I caught myself just in time to resist saying, "The Indian! How silly! That was just an actor in a film and nothing to feel bad about!" Instead I accepted his perception of the incident and just gave the comfort he needed.

Once he had verbalized his distress and I had responded with acceptance, the trauma was over and I could tell that the communication bridge between us was beginning to be rebuilt. I have been so thankful I didn't thoughtlessly put down his self-expression and stifle the very thing I was trying to encourage.

It is amazing that we can live in the same country, speak the same language, even live in the same house, yet struggle to communicate with one another. Part of the reason this is such a challenge is that communication occurs in many forms and our minds respond to the incoming messages so differently.

Communication may be visual, such as a frown at a little hand reaching for the fourth piece of candy from Grandma's candy dish. It may be written, such as a note tucked into a first-grader's lunch box

*S*ilence with acceptance can be a valuable aid to communication.

saying "I love you." Or it may be through physical action, such as when we give a child a hug.

In any situation, each of us notice and remember different things. Some of us are tuned in to visual cues, others to sound, yet others to physical actions. For one child, hearing "I love you" is very meaningful. Another child will remember a hug longer than any spoken words. Our responsibility as parents is to understand what kind of communication our children respond to the most, then use that form as a bridge for building our relationships.

To determine which type of communication is most meaningful to your children, consider the verbs and adjectives they use to express themselves. For example, a child may indicate comprehension of an idea by saying, "Oh I see!" "I hear you," or "Now I get it," indicating a focus on sight, sound, or action words. Don't hesitate to ask your children what is most meaningful to them. They may not know right away, but as they think about it they should be able to tell you what communicates most to them.

During this month you want to focus on teaching your children to communicate—and teaching yourself to really hear them when they do. Poor communication is a common cause of difficulty between friends, on the job, and at home. So anything you can do to help your children develop healthy communication skills will benefit them.

SCRIPTURE

What a privilege it is to learn about communication from God, our Creator and the Master Communicator. He designed a fascinating array of ways for his creatures, great and small, to communicate with one another. These methods range from the chemical trail left by the first ant at your picnic or the flick of a frightened deer's tail, to man's spoken communication or body language.

God chose to share himself with man, his highest creation. He revealed himself to Jacob, who dreamily watched a ladder stretching up into heaven; and to a crowd of Israelites who stood by Moses as he spoke to a rock and water gushed out; and to Gideon, who knelt on a threshing floor squeezing the moisture from a dew-soaked fleece.

After 1500 years of visions and prophetic writings, God's supreme commitment to communication is summarized in John 1:14: "The Word became flesh and dwelt among us."

It is interesting to study Christ's ministry and see how he bridged the gap between himself and mankind. He spit into mud, made clay, and reached out to touch the eyes of one blind man. For the Centurion whose servant was sick with palsy, the spoken word was enough. To doubting Thomas, Christ held out his hands for inspection. How blessed we are to know this master communicator and to let our children know that he will be their friend.

As you teach communication skills this month, be sure to encourage your children to learn to communicate with God. When they are old enough to read books by themselves, they are ready for a personal devotional time. You can help them by getting a Bible or devotional book for them to read, and helping them plan a time and place for them to pray uninterrupted.

Here are four Scriptures from Proverbs for your children to learn this month. They focus on verbal communication and on the power the spoken word has to hurt or heal.

"A wholesome tongue is a tree of life" (Proverbs 15:4).

"A word fitly spoken is like apples of gold in settings of silver" (Proverbs 25:11).

"Death and life are in the power of the tongue" (Proverbs 18:21).

"The tongue of the wise uses knowledge rightly" (Proverbs 15:2).

Remember, as you work with your children on communication you need to model this last Scripture for them. It is not enough to see your children's faults and the places they need improvement, then tell them to shape up. Wisdom will help you use that knowledge "rightly" to find encouraging, supportive ways to bring about change. Your children need your support and encouragement, not your constant criticism.

SLOGANS

Here are three short slogans to use when you are teaching your child the character quality of communication:

- I Can Share Myself with Words.
- Kindness Is in the Tone of Voice.
- A Hug a Day Keeps the Doctor Away.

Maybe we need a new bumper sticker that asks, "Have you hugged your dad and mom today?" Your children need to learn that you need hugs, too!

ACTIVITIES

The most important thing you could do this month to help develop communication would be to establish a "family time" once a week. Nothing you can give your children compares with the gift of yourself and your time. If you begin doing this when the children are small, it will build bonds of understanding and family unity that will weather the winds of adolescence. It has not been easy making and keeping a commitment to family time in the fast-paced life on Florida's Gold Coast (nor would it be anywhere else in the United States), but the long-term benefits are worth the effort.

A real family time needs to meet several specific criteria. First, it should be at the same time each week so both Dad and Mom can remember to make plans around that specific block of time. It may be Friday night, Monday afternoon, or whatever works best in your home, but it should be scheduled consistently and protected as a valuable family treasure. If you as parents value it, your children will, too. They will be very jealous of anything interfering with that time together.

Second, no one else should be invited to join you. Family time is not a time to socialize with others. You cannot have valuable interaction with your children if another couple is along. You end up interacting with the other adults and virtually ignoring your children. So, family time should be a time alone with just your family.

Third, the activities for the evening should be mutually enjoyable to all family members, especially the children. Our family times have included a cookout at the park, gathering shells on the beach, a trip to the mall, reading a book together, playing games, planning an upcoming vacation, and walking a mile or so down the railroad tracks together.

On our railroad track expedition, the whole family (with dog in tow) walked about a mile down the tracks in our town. We collected wild flowers, old spikes, and a rodent skeleton—a truly profitable evening in our youngest son's opinion! (On the negative side, we were almost run over by a train! It's amazing how little sound you hear from an approaching train when it is directly in front of you. So take care if your family goes on such an excursion!)

When you run out of ideas for family time activities, have each family member write three suggestions on separate slips of paper and put them in a cookie jar. Then before the next family day let one of the children pull out a slip of paper, and make plans to do whatever is written on it.

If these hours together are going to be enjoyable, the time must be freely given; both Dad and Mom must be happy to be with the children. We began a consistent family time when our boys were eight and five years old. It was quite a struggle at first, with the other demands on our time. One evening returning from our time together, my husband announced as we pulled into the driveway, "Well, I hope you enjoyed that!" There was a moment of silence in the car, then a small voice from the back seat asked, "Did you enjoy it? I want you to enjoy it, too!" We realized a true family time would be done with our children, not at them!

A great deal of communication is nonverbal, so learn to read your children's silent messages.

Your children are going to have an impact on you as long as you live, so I hope you will make a serious effort to begin a family time, starting this month. It will be the greatest investment in family unity and communication you can make, for it lets your children know they are important enough to you to receive your most valuable possessions: yourself and your time.

In addition to a family time, there are some other activities you and your children can try this month. Look them over and decide which ones will fit your family best.

Two to Seven Years Old

For some youngsters verbal expression is no problem; they can talk continuously. A simple trip to a grocery store is accompanied by a barrage of unanswerable questions. "Who is the lady in that car?" "Where is she going?" "Why is she going there?" "Is she going to the grocery store, too?"

There aren't usually easy answers to these questions either! If you absentmindedly say, "Yes, she's going to the store," the kid wants to know what she is going to buy! And if you say, "No, she's not going to the store," you must give a lawyer's defense of why not.

Since listening is half of communication, youngsters like this need help in learning to listen. Here are five steps to teach them this skill:

1. Have them repeat instructions after you give them.

2. Have them repeat reassurances once they have been given. When my oldest child was a toddler he was distressed any time I left him, so I began to tell him again and again before I left, "Mommy be back!" And I had him repeat the words. Soon he joyously greeted my arrival calling, "Mommy back, Mommy back!"

3. See that your children don't interrupt you when you are talking. But don't expect them to wait much more than ten seconds for your attention—they just can't do it when they are little. They will learn to wait if you respond to them quickly.

4. Have them explain a concept you have shared. If you answered the question, "Where is God?" or "Why can't I see God?" have them repeat the answer after you give it.

5. Have them practice times of silence. This isn't always easy, but periodic practice sessions lasting thirty seconds to two minutes will help a great deal. Our oldest child was a typical talkative youngster. When Nathan was born my mother came to stay with us and take care of Philip, who was then three and a half. One day she took him to the store, and he talked getting in the car, the whole way to the store, and as they walked into the store.

As she started down the first aisle Grandma said, "Philip, you have talked a long time. Now, can you be quiet while I try to think of what I need to buy?" Philip exercised great restraint and remained silent all the way down that first aisle. When he reached the end he could contain himself no longer and wanted to know, "Can I talk now?"

As you develop communication skills, you need some specific goals in mind. One of these goals should be for your children to learn to convey information accurately. There are a number of exercises you can do to help them learn how to do this. As you do these different exercises with the children, explain to them that their goal in conveying information is to keep it clear, concise, complete, and correct.

1. Have the children practice telling you how to get to the grocery store, school, or Grandma's house. All of us who have asked for directions in a strange town realize how many adults lack the ability to convey accurate information. Your daughter needs to be able to give her friend directions when she is going to come over to play. And your son should be able to tell his friend's mom how to take him home after T-ball practice.

Practicing giving directions can be an enjoyable bedtime exercise. If you diagram the directions on a piece of paper, it lets all of you see the information conveyed by specific words.

2. When the family plays a simple game like UNO, let the children take turns trying to tell the group how it is played. This will increase their skill in choosing words for expressing particular ideas.

3. Give the children a chance during play time to explain how to perform a physical task. For example, after you have explained how to throw a ball or swing the bat, have them explain the process back to you as you follow their instructions carefully.

4. Creative storytelling is an area in which some children should be encouraged. As you fix supper, have your four- or five-year-old sit at the table and tell you a Bible story, bedtime story, or some tale of their own making. An oatmeal box with the end cut out adds resonance to the voice and makes exercising the imagination more fun.

5. Teach your children how to share events in time. The ability to describe the sequence of events is necessary for children to share an experience they had with friends or family members.

Have Dad begin by telling about his day during supper. He should include interesting highlights, such as, "I got up early (or late). On the way to work the traffic was light (or there was an accident at the corner or Green Street and Gunnison downtown). The first thing we did was have an office meeting to plan for summer. I saw Tom at lunch—remember you met him at the lake last year? He asked about you all," etc.

Then let one of the children have a turn. Help them learn how to put events in a time sequence by the questions you ask. "What happened first today? What did you do next? Did you do art before you went to lunch?"

A second concern you should have for your children is that they learn how to express emotion. There are several ways to help them accomplish this.

1. Explain your own emotions to your children. Suppose you are sitting on the couch, crying, a half-read letter in your lap, and your children come in and ask, "What is wrong, Mom?"

If your response is, "Oh, nothing really," you miss the chance to illustrate how to express emotions by your example. Should this happen often, their conclusion may be that emotions should not be verbalized.

It would be much better to wipe a tear away and say, "I am sad about what my friend Sue wrote in this letter. Do you remember Sue, Bill, and the girls who were here last summer? Well, little Lisa is very sick in the hospital, and that makes me sad."

2. Teach your children to channel emotion into constructive useful action. In the illustration given above, you might decide to send a get-well card to Lisa and have the children draw pictures to include in the card. Or you might decide to pray together for your friend's sick child.

If you encounter a political problem, consider writing a letter to the local commissioner, and having the children address the envelope and put the letter in the mailbox when you are finished.

3. Have your children take turns explaining or expressing emotions. Ask questions such as, "How does sad look?" "How does sad act?" "What does sad think?" Then move on to other emotion words such as "love," "security," or "happiness" and work with the different aspects of these emotions. Remember, no one is wrong in his expression, as long as he is really trying to communicate.

A third goal to work on this month is helping your children express abstract ideas. Here are a few ways to encourage this in your children.

1. Play the Ungame with your family. This is a wonderful game by The Ungame Company in Anaheim, California. It has several sets of cards with questions such as "How would you describe a happy family?"

"What is love?" "Say something about beauty," or "What is faith?" It is called the "ungame" because no one wins and no one loses; the objective is to stir thoughtful communication by each player.

2. Include discussion of ideas in your supper-time conversation. Talk about current events so your children learn your political perspective. Discuss tenets of your faith so your children can ask about prayer, baptism, and salvation. Share your reactions to art and architecture so they learn a basis for evaluation.

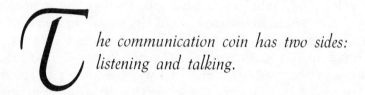

The communication coin has two sides: listening and talking.

Eight to Fifteen Years Old

Now you are ready to work on the finer points of communication. At this age, you need to explain to the children what you are working on and why. They will enjoy the project more if they understand the importance and purpose of the different exercises.

1. Help your children understand a disagreement from the other person's point of view. For example, let's say your younger daughter borrowed her older sister's sweater without asking. She doesn't understand why her older sister gets upset when she finds out about the borrowed sweater. The daughter who borrowed the sweater needs to be able to move from her defensive position and consider her sister's position. Perhaps the older sister hasn't even worn the sweater yet, or maybe it was a birthday gift from someone special, or whatever. Help each party in a disagreement to see both sides of a situation.

When there is a disagreement in your family, stop the "discussion" that is taking place and explain that before it continues, those involved are going to do an exercise in communication. Have them "trade sides." Tell one child to explain how the other child feels—what she thinks and why—as completely as she can. Then have the other child do the same, arguing her sibling's case without lapsing back into her own attitudes and reactions.

2. Teach your children to think about a situation from a perspective completely outside of it. An adult listening to two teenagers argue has a very different view of the situation than the people involved.

To help your children develop a different perspective, stop the two young people and ask them one at a time to move physically to your position in the room, shut their eyes, and mentally or verbally replay the conversation that just occurred, complete with expressions, and physical actions. The best result from this is that the confrontation may appear so funny from the new vantage point that it brings on gales of laughter. But even if this doesn't happen, your children will learn how to remove themselves from the heat of the moment and try to get an "outsider's" perspective on what is happening.

3. No matter how convinced your children are about what was said or done in a situation, they must learn that their perception of reality is exactly that: their perception. It is not necessarily reality.

Once your children begin to realize this, they can learn to resist the impulse to say, "No, that isn't what happened!" when they hear their brother's explanation of an event. They will understand that their brother is telling the chain of events as he sees them. So a proper response from them is, "That's interesting, I thought it happened this way," or "As nearly as I remember it, it happened that way."

Even adults have a difficult time accepting the fact that they (or their spouses) are not "right" and the other person "wrong." In many situations people on both sides see some aspects of truth or reality. Usually neither of them has the whole picture. Just realizing this helps us listen to what the other person is saying from a new frame of reference, trying to understand what the other person's reality is rather than disprove them.

However, to help someone incorporate new information or viewpoints into his perspective, you must discover his starting point, what he believes or thinks about something. The next step is to accept his reality as truth to him. There aren't many people who think, "I know what I am thinking is wrong, but I'm going to think it anyway!" Most of us are convinced what we think is true and our way of thinking is the right way. That's fine as long as we know that the people we are trying to communicate with most probably are not thinking the same as we are, and they are equally convinced they have truth.

Good communication relies on understanding both sides of an issue and negotiating to reach a resolution. It is crucial for parents working with teenagers to understand this. The teenager who says, "All you ever do is nag at me, you never appreciate anything I do!" believes what she is saying is true. (And if you cannot remember several times in the last month when you expressed appreciation to your teenager for something she did, she may have a point that needs your consideration!) A parent's frontal attack declaring, "That's not true!" is as pointless here as it is with the kid who says, "No one ever wants to play with me!" You must give illustrations of contradictory evidence if you are to move them from their subjective reality to a broader, more accurate one.

4. Teach your children how to have a "discussion" instead of an "argument." If you can use the technique given below with your children, there will be little friction in your home. Also, they will learn valuable skills to use with their peers, on the job, and later in marriage.

First decide on the goal of the discussion. Is it just to blow off steam, expressing hurt or anger? If so, that can happen anytime and anywhere. If all you want to do is blow up and you don't care who you hurt in the process or if your relationship is damaged, you will need little preparation other than a lung full of air!

However, if your goal is to change attitudes or actions, that is quite something else. Real communication, communication that is not just emotional eruptions, will take more effort. Here are six steps you can take to achieve real communication in your family.

First, plan a time to talk. Some people are morning people; they are ready to handle problems at 8 A.M. Other people are night people; they can't constructively cope with life before noon. These differences in people are biochemical realities, not just excuses for laziness. Peak performance hours are tied to body temperature, enzyme activity, and basal metabolic rate. These biochemical characteristics vary from person to person. The labels "night owl" or "early bird" arise from these physiological differences in our biological clocks.

The children and adults in a family need to be aware of the other members' biological clocks, and plan discussion time when both parties are awake, clothed, and in their right minds.

Second, choose a setting. Remember your goal is a change of behavior, not just the venting of emotions. Be willing to wait for the most appropriate, pleasant, productive setting.

You can teach your children through your example to plan discussion time. Has your daughter arrived home at 12:30 A.M. when she promised to be in at 11 P.M.? Tell her you are glad she is home safely and that you will talk to her tomorrow. (If your emotions are too high to permit sleep, get up and write down what you would like to say to her. Writing your thoughts down does get them "off your mind.")

The best setting may be going on a walk together or having a Coke at the local diner. A public place may be more conducive to remembering consideration and good manners than the foyer at home. Once you've chosen a setting, get a paper and pencil for both of you.

Third, as the discussion begins, take turns talking. Let the young person go first, or the person who is upset and called for the conference. The most important ground rule is: *No interruptions allowed.*

This is where the paper and pencil come in. Each person should jot down notes about anything the other person says that he or she feels needs clarification, explanation, or comment. But remember, *no interruptions!*

Fourth, really listen to what is being said. Accept the fact that right now this person believes everything she is saying. Put yourself in her place, feel her hurts, and accept her perspective as truth to her. If you believed the people and situations were as this person describes them, what would you do? How would you deal with the type of person she describes you to be—after all, that's who you are to her!

Fifth, let the other person talk. Again we have only writing and no interruptions. One turn per person may be enough, or you may have to have two uninterrupted rounds before you are ready for open discussion.

Sixth, conclude the time together with each of you agreeing to work on changes. Select the one or two most important changes the other person would like to see take place, and work on them.

This format is for major discussions, and if it is used periodically, it will greatly minimize tension in relationships. Then the little problems can be handled on a less dramatic scale.

Be tuned in to your children's communication time; they may not be ready to listen when you are ready to lecture.

5. Teach your children how to make an apology. The child or adult who can say, "I'm sorry, I was wrong," will defuse resentment and be more able to get along with those around him. (The greatest tool you have for teaching this lesson is through your own example. You need to be able to admit your mistakes and apologize, too—even to your children!)

6. Many young people are insecure about holding a conversation with adults or with members of the opposite sex. Your children will be most appreciative if you will help them overcome these fears. Explain to them that the first step is to look people in the eye during a conversation.

To initiate a conversation they should use common ground to get the conversational ball rolling. If they are going to or coming from a school class, a ball game, or church service, this will provide a common topic for discussion.

Then they need to be willing to listen and respond to questions or comments. A conversation is like a game of catch, the conversational ball needs to be tossed back and forth. No one should do all the talking. (*Man in Demand,* written by Wayne and Emily Hunter and published by Harvest House Publishers, is a workbook for young men. It has excellent suggestions for developing conversational skills.)

Another conversation starter can be compliments. If your child has just received a compliment for something, such as playing the piano or singing, he should look the other person in the eye and say "Thank you." Then he can ask if the other person plays or sings. In this way he can once again find a common ground.

7. Handling business transactions is another conversational skill your children should learn. Whether they do baby-sitting or lawn-mowing, they need to know what to say and what not to say. They should know how to discuss payment, whether to let the "employer" decide or to simply charge an hourly rate, before they begin work. They need to consider and agree on hours and a set time as to when the job is ended. Discussing these criteria with them will increase their self-confidence and conversational skills.

8. Finally, teach your children how to appeal to authority. This will be a valuable communication tool for interacting with teachers, employers, and even parents.

When appealing to authority, your children should first express confidence in that individual by saying, "I know you have my best interests at heart." Then they need to explain their position, "I want to go here, buy this, or do that because. . . ." After that they can put in an appeal, "This means a lot to me because my best friend is going," or "I have wanted to buy one for three years," and so on.

They should end their appeal by the commitment, "I will abide by whatever decision you make." Children can be comfortable with such a commitment, especially if they have learned they always have access to a higher court of appeal. God declares, "The king's heart is in the hand of the Lord, like the rivers of water; He turns it wherever He wishes" (Proverbs 21:1). If you make a wrong decision, God can help you realize it. He can do the same with others in authority over your children, too, if it is his will and they trust in him.

Chapter Ten. Purity: Valuing Myself and Others by Guarding My Thoughts and Actions

"When all else fails, read the directions!" These instructions often are included by manufacturers when they pack expensive instruments. They also can be applied to people and the problem of purity.

Some psychologists told us thirty years ago that all of society's problems would be solved if we would just get rid of our Victorian restraints. Purity was out unless it was something you wanted. There was no right or wrong. There was only "freedom" from restrictions. So we complied—and the problems of promiscuity, divorce, desertion, pornography, and sexual abuse of children skyrocketed.

What about the people? Are they any better off after "freeing" themselves from the restriction of purity? Quite to the contrary, as we ignored God and his guidelines for living there seem to be more blighted and unhappy people than ever before.

Let's face it, God created us. He knows how we are designed emotionally, and he gave us specific directions for conducting interpersonal relationships, especially those between men and women. Too often, humanistic counselors, like Satan in the garden, picture God as one who would deprive man of knowledge and pleasure. Yet all their words and assurances cannot nullify the devastating effects of ignoring God's instructions. The truth is, the only thing God seeks to deprive us of is physical and emotional pain.

The problems of the Victorian era were not the result of living according to God's guidelines. The problems came from trying to live by God's rules without a heart committed to him and a willingness to let his grace reign in every area of life.

It seems we have enough evidence to prove that the humanistic solution hasn't worked. In fact, we are in worse shape than ever! Everything the world has recommended—sex education, birth control pills, unrestricted sex—has failed. So isn't it time to read the directions from the original manufacturer? He understands better than anyone the delicate balance between human physical needs, emotional needs, and sense of self-worth.

And his ways are *not* restrictive! Rather, they are the only ways we can find true joy and freedom in the lives he has given us.

The mother of a sweet fifteen-year-old girl in our congregation recently shared with me a question her daughter had asked: "Mom, why should I wait until marriage to have sex? What difference does it make anyway?"

What difference does it make?

That is a question that deserves an answer, and you as a parent must be prepared to give that answer. Whether or not your children are brave enough to ask it out loud, you may be sure they are asking it within themselves.

So, what difference does it make?

First, following God's guidelines for purity makes a world of difference in our sense of self-worth.

True intimacy is always tied to a degree of interpersonal commitment. It may be as shallow and brief as, "You're the most exciting person I've ever met!" But whatever method or words are used, people single each other out in an expression of mutual admiration and a relationship begins. Should the light of another day find the friend or lover in the arms of another, a sense of betrayal is inevitable—and betrayal is followed by a reevaluation of self-worth and desirability.

When we insist that commitment shouldn't matter, we ignore the fabric of our personalities. Commitment does and always will matter. There is no "free" love. The only free thing is the costly destruction of our self-worth.

Second, following God's laws for purity makes a difference in our self-confidence. In the "Manufacturer's" design, our self-confidence was intended to blossom and mature within the security of a permanent relationship.

When I taught part-time at a local public college, I was saddened to hear the girls talk about, "My roommate, he . . ." It wasn't "my boyfriend," just "my roommate." However when someone came to class with a new engagement ring, everyone was happy and excited. The most frequently-made comment was, "That's commitment!" Despite the negative publicity marriage has received, these insecure young women with "roommates" recognized something of value when they saw it—the security of marriage.

Third, purity makes a difference in our sense of self-confidence. Many young people are like the young man who wrote to Dear Abby several years ago. He was in his early teens and his first romantic involvement with a girlfriend escalated to the point of sexual intimacy. Within a few weeks the girl quit seeing him. His sense of self-confidence and self-esteem was devastated. The resolve he wrote about in his letter to Abby was a determination to reserve future sexual intimacy until he was ready for the commitment of marriage.

Fourth, being sexually pure makes a difference in our health. Years ago the fear of syphilis and gonorrhea helped deter young people when tempted to indulge in intimacy before marriage. Then, with the advent of penicillin and other drugs, that fear faded. (It is interesting, though, that while medication eliminates the initial infection, the antibodies for those diseases remain in the blood forever. So a blood test always reveals that the person once contracted a sexual disease.)

Now AIDS (Acquired Immune Deficiency Syndrome) is a very real and deadly threat. The world doesn't like to hear it, but it is still true: God is not mocked and his principles for living cannot be ignored without tragic effects. It's like anything else, whatever you do has consequences. In accepting the lies about purity, we have gotten ourselves into some very serious trouble.

Fifth, purity makes a difference in future relationships. According to statistics from marriage counselors, young people who wait until marriage for physical intimacy have a much better chance for a stable, enduring relationship, one that is built on mutual trust and respect.

Sixth, purity makes a difference in your relationship with God. Sexual intimacy, except between men and women within the bond of marriage, is forbidden by Scripture (despite modern theological attempts to twist the Word). Enough vestiges of right and wrong still permeate our society that people know immorality is wrong. When young couples who are living together get saved, the first concern they usually express is the need to get married.

So the answer to the question "What difference does it make?" is that involvement in sexual intimacy outside of marriage destroys the very things young people are hoping for in their relationships: emotional security, a strong sense of self-worth and self-esteem, and closeness with the spouse and with God.

(For further help in answering this question for your children, consider purchasing Josh McDowell's book *Why Wait?* and the magazine/book *Heartbeat* from Tyndale House Publishers.)

SCRIPTURE

Scriptures for your children to learn this month as you emphasize purity are:

"Your body is the temple of the Holy Spirit" (1 Corinthians 6:19).

"Keep yourself pure" (1 Timothy 5:22).

"Honor God with your body" (1 Corinthians 6:20).

There is no such thing as "free" love, the only thing free is the costly destruction of our self-worth.

"Who can find a virtuous wife? For her worth is far above rubies. The heart of her husband safely trusts her; so he will have no lack of gain" (Proverbs 31:10-11).

"Whatever is pure . . . think about such things" (Philippians 4:8, NIV).

The first battleground for purity is in the mind, so you must teach your children to guard their minds if they are to be morally pure. They can guard their minds by being careful what they look at. Have your children ever seen pornographic pictures? How will you know if you do not ask them? By asking your children about this, you give them opportunity to confess if they have come across such materials. Confession will bring relief if such a guilty secret is harassing them. And if it isn't dealt with, it will short-circuit your efforts to teach about moral purity.

However, don't be angry with your children for making such a confession. It should be a time of mutually shared sorrow that Satan tried to establish a foothold in their minds. Comfort them and let them know that God can help give freedom from those mental images if they want it. End the discussion with a warning to protect themselves in the future, and with a time of prayer for God's cleansing and help.

Recently I heard a young Christian father insist, "All boys look at pornography if they get a chance." He had seen lewd magazines as a child, so he assumed his own boys would take the opportunity to peruse such material if it was available. But your children can be warned about pornography, which will prepare them to get away from pictures they may see or their friends may try to show them. They won't know to avoid such material unless you prepare them ahead of time, helping them understand how they should react.

You also need to keep a close check on the books your children read. When one of our sons was nine, he got the book *Run, Baby, Run* by Nicky Cruz off of our bookshelf while we were away and began to read it. When he told us what he was reading, the book was vetoed as inappropriate for him at his age. Unfortunately, he had already read descriptions of some of the boy-girl relationships that existed in the street gangs of New York. He understood why we said it was inappropriate, and was sorry about the word pictures painted in his mind. Since that time he has been very careful to guard his mind from any questionable reading material, and we have tried to be more careful about what is available to the boys.

SLOGANS

It is never too early to begin teaching both your sons and daughters the importance of purity as a special treasure. Once purity of the soul is lost a measure of innocence is gone that can never be regained. Immorality is a blight on the soul, like soil on a garment. Such garments are put on sale at reduced prices. Even after the cleansing of God's forgiveness, many young people struggle with the temptation to sell themselves at bargain basement prices. How much better it is to spare your children such a struggle.

The compounded tragedy of promiscuity is it can make it doubly hard for parents with this problem in their past to talk to their children about moral purity. If you have made mistakes in this area of your life you know the pain it causes. Accept God's forgiveness and healing, and be diligent to warn and protect your children so they will be spared what you have suffered.

Here are three slogans to use this month as you concentrate on purity:

- Moral Purity Is God's Standard.
- The Battle for Purity Is Won In My Mind.
- Moral Purity Is a Precious Treasure.

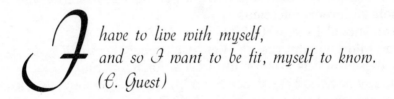

I have to live with myself,
and so I want to be fit, myself to know.
(E. Guest)

ACTIVITIES

Two to Seven Years Old

Let's approach your activities for this month by answering some of the questions commonly asked by young parents.

1. "How old should my children be before I explain to them the facts of life?"

The answer generally given is, "That depends on the child." However, you do need to talk with your children sometime after three and before seven years of age. Seven may seem young, but if you wait much longer you may be like Bob, a college friend of my husband. Bob's oldest son had just turned nine, and he had decided it was time to have a man-to-man talk with him. The boy's reaction to his father's attempt was, "Oh, I already know all about that. The neighbor kid told me a long time ago!"

If you believe such topics are the parents' prerogative, you had better beat "the neighbor kid" to explaining life and love to your children. But if you find the neighbor children have already established an information bureau, don't give up. Have your children share what they have heard. In all likelihood they have been recipients of a great deal of misinformation, and you at least might set the record straight.

When you do talk to your children about sex, end each discussion with the reminder that they are not to talk about this with their friends. Tell them you will answer any questions they have, and other children's parents will answer their children's questions.

2. "What kind of words should I use to talk about sex?"

When you talk to your children about their bodies, use proper terminology. A two-year-old may have a "wa-wee," but a seven-year-old needs a more adult term for his penis.

Most young parents today have had the benefit of a high-school biology discussion on reproduction, so they have some exposure to reproductive terms. You will find using proper terms helps you if the topic is uncomfortable for you. It also makes the discussion more academic and less personal.

3. "Do I answer only the questions my child asks?"

Have you ever sat in an audience where the speaker handled a complicated topic and then asked, "Are there any questions?" Most of the time the audience is silent!

It takes a certain amount of knowledge to ask an intelligent question. Your children may not even know what to ask. When your children ask questions is certainly a good time to answer them. But most parents are caught off-guard when children ask them about their bodies and sex. Sometimes a response on this topic requires a bit of psychological preparation.

Let me illustrate. It was quite easy, with one of our boys, to explain the facts of life. But with the other it seemed I shared less and made little progress when I tried. The evening this realization dawned on me, I felt obligated to remedy the situation promptly.

So, the next day I told my son I had something very important to talk to him about, and we settled ourselves on the living room couch. I reviewed male and female anatomy, talked about marriage, explained the process of fertilization of an egg, told how babies were born, and ended with an admonition for moral purity. My son squirmed and fidgeted, but I persevered.

When I finally finished he turned to me and said, "Yes, Mom. Now can we talk about something really important? Like, can I have a train for Christmas?"

I mentally threw my hands in the air and thought, "No wonder I feel like I haven't communicated with this child!"

However, he was listening more than I realized. Several weeks had passed and the family was out getting hamburgers one family night. My son carried his tray to a table, set it down, then turned toward me as I threaded my way through the tables toward him. With a perplexed look on his face (and with what sounded to me like an awfully loud voice) he asked, "Mom, how did you say it was that the sperm got there?"

From that experience I learned two valuable lessons. First, I didn't have to worry about telling my child too much. What was meaningful would stick—the rest would blow over his head like leaves in a breeze. Second, I learned that although I thought I could handle the topic comfortably, my preference was to arrange a setting for such questions!

If you are waiting for your children to ask before you discuss some subjects, you had better be prepared for some less than ideal situations! I encourage you to choose your own setting when the time is right.

4. "How do I discuss the topic of sexuality without embarrassing myself, or my son or daughter?"

In most households the parent most comfortable with this topic is usually the one to discuss it. Often this is the mother, simply because she is around the children more and opportunities for discussion are greater. But this is an increasingly important question as the number of single parent households grow. In our congregation of two hundred we have three fathers who are single parents, and two of them have daughters.

In our home the boys feel free to talk about any of these issues with their father. But since I teach college biology and deal with the subject of reproduction in the classroom each year, it has been natural for me to talk to the boys about it.

Don't let your uncertainties or discomfort in this area cause you to be like many parents who shirk their responsibility, protesting, "I don't know if I can answer my children's questions." Or like the forty-year-old mother of a late-in-life child who, giggling and blushing, said, "Oh, I could never talk to my son about something like that!"

If you are not comfortable with the subject, help yourself out! Go to a used bookstore and pick up a college biology book for a couple of dollars. (A new one costs about forty dollars!) Try to get a book not more than ten years old. While human anatomy hasn't changed in the last twenty years, the topics discussed have!

Look over the chapter on "Reproduction" before you buy the book. It should have drawings of male and female anatomy, a discussion of the physiology of intercourse, diagrams of the menstrual cycle, and a section on how different birth control devices work. It should also give pertinent facts about sexual diseases, though you probably won't find many used books that address AIDS. AIDS is too recent a problem to be covered in an older book. In newer texts it may be discussed in the chapter on "Reproduction" or in the one on "Immunity."

Reading these books will help you review proper terminology and basic information and will prepare you to sit down and use the impersonal diagrams to study and discuss the subject with your children. However, these books will not provide a moral framework for this information. That will be entirely up to you! Along with a textbook, you may want to get a book like *The Wonderful Way That Babies Are Made* by Larry Christenson. It will help you develop a moral context for the discussion.

The single father may feel too uncomfortable to discuss sexuality with his daughter, and may ask a family friend to help him. But he needs to leave the door for confidence open by explaining, "I have asked Mrs. So-and-so to talk with you about this topic because she may be able to answer your questions better than I can. But I will help you in any way I can as you are in this process of growing up."

My experience has been that children view the subject objectively rather than personalizing it. If your relationship with them is a normal healthy one, then they generally will separate the discussion from themselves and you.

5. "Should I tell my child the sexual experience is fun?"

If you have taught your children personal modesty, they will naturally recoil from the intimacy involved in procreation. (I remember amusing comments like, "Well, you might have to do that once or twice in your life to have children, but that's all!")

The compounded tragedy of abuse and promiscuity is that they prevent many parents from protecting their children from the same problems.

Every form of American media is shouting the delights of premarital sex. It is your job to instill in your children the truth that a physical relationship is only really fun, satisfying, and non-destructive to the human personality when it takes place inside the bond of marriage.

6. "What can I do to protect my children from being molested?"

This is one question every parent should ask. There are several things you can do. The first is pray for your children's protection; the second is pay attention to your intuition! A friend who is a psychiatrist once remarked, "Your intuition will be right about 95 percent of the time, so pay attention to it! If you have a feeling that something is wrong about a situation, you are probably right."

Third, you should know where your children are and who they are with. There are potential dangers for your children everywhere, from the church nursery to a family get-together. It is so easy when visiting family and friends to relax and let the children play. But Dad and Mom, you need to check where your children are, who they are with, and what's going on. Just the fact that you do check and veto closed doors and secluded places will warn off some would-be predators. The old saying "an ounce of prevention is worth a pound of cure" is certainly true in this area. Authorities continue to warn that children are usually fondled or molested by family members or close family friends—so you cannot be too careful.

A fourth step you can take to protect your daughters is to be concerned about how they are dressed. Civil authorities used to warn parents as summer approached that the incidence of rape and child molesting increased dramatically in the summer when children were more scantily clad. Don't let the world dictate fashion to you and your children. Just good common sense warns that a style like a bare midriff can be an invitation for exploring hands.

The world has thumbed its nose at modesty, considering it an archaic concept, but we are paying a tragically high price for such willful disregard. Disbelief in gravity does not nullify its effects, and immodesty still excites interest and desire.

One mother moaned to my husband recently after a very unfortunate incident at a swimming pool, "I wish someone had warned me before about dressing my little girl this way in front of teenage boys. I just didn't even think about it."

The best thing you can do to help protect your children is talk, talk, talk to them. The talking needs to include questions and warnings. Ask your children if anyone has ever tried to get them to take off their clothes. Warn them if this happens to say a big loud "No!" and run to tell you. Tell them that their bodies are their property, and no one else's. No one can touch them if they don't want them to. Discuss the differences between "right touch" and "wrong touch." Encourage them to listen to their intuition, too. If they are uncomfortable or frightened in any situation, regardless of who is involved (friends, relatives, teachers . . . even parents!) tell them to use their big loud "No!" and, once again, come to you. Preparation ahead of time for this emergency will enable your children to act when otherwise they most likely would be frightened into immobility.

Ask your children if they are uncomfortable around or afraid of any adult. Encourage them to tell you if they are ever around someone who makes them feel uncomfortable. An incident where our boys hid on the floor in the back seat of the car when a man who had been a family friend approached warned us about an abnormal situation.

Ask your child if any older child or adult has shown them pictures or done something to or with them, then told them not to tell you. Encourage them that if something like this ever happens they are to tell you

*D*on't wait too long to teach your children about sexuality and purity. If you do, the neighbor children will establish an information bureau.

right away. Let them know they never need to have secrets from their parents.

I have deliberately suggested asking questions before giving warnings because it may be easier to get a response from a small child that way. Be sure to reassure your children that if these things happen you will not be angry with them. After all, they will not have done anything wrong. Let them know that you want to protect them and you will see that they are not around people who frighten them.

7. "What shall I do if my child is molested?"

Sadly, this last question confronts more and more parents every day. Counseling young women in high school and college who are dealing with the ongoing trauma of such an experience has made me realize that parents must be better prepared to help them cope with such a tragedy.

Molestation or abuse usually happens when a child is small and easily intimidated. Depending on the extent of the violation, the child may not really comprehend the significance of the event until they are ten or eleven years old. When they do understand it, it is suddenly as if the incident happens all over again.

Several years ago, a college girl told me how she experienced this double trauma. I asked her if she had talked to her mother about the situation when she realized what had happened. Her response was, "Yes, and that is the worst part of it all! She just ignored the whole thing and told me to forget it! I've never been able to forgive her for that. What does it matter what I do now? I'm already no good!"

You can prepare to help your child by realizing that no matter how small a child is, the events surrounding a violation of their person are captured forever in their minds. You will not eliminate the problem by ignoring it or making light of it. If the neighborhood bully slapped your child or pushed her down, you would give comfort and support. If your child has been fondled or sexually assaulted, he or she needs to grieve with you and have you share in the pain.

After comforting your child, you need to reassure her (or him) that she did not cause this to happen. It was caused by sin in the other person's life. Ask your child how she would feel if someone stole her purse. Probably angry, but would she feel like a thief? I'm sure not. If someone lied to her, would that make her a liar? No, of course not. Then she can be assured that someone else doing wrong does not make her bad.

One note: parents with daughters aren't the only ones who should be concerned. If you have sons, you need to be tuned in to having the same concern and care for them. Our society is not one that discriminates between the sexes when it comes to abuse or molestation. Boys are in as much danger as girls.

In summary, there are several activities you need to do this month to help your younger children develop purity:

1. Get a college biology book and review the basic anatomy and physiology of reproduction. If the children are not too small, the trip to the bookstore could be a family time activity.

2. Talk with your children several different times about the topics mentioned above. Explain the reproductive process. Ask your children questions and give them warnings about molestation or abuse.

3. Most important of all, pray daily for God's protection over your children, that he will help them remain pure and keep them safe.

Eight to Fifteen Years Old

If you have done your homework, your children already know the basic facts of life by the time they reach this age. Now you are ready to help them develop purity as a goal for their personal lives. You can do this in several ways.

1. When our son was seventeen he came home from school one day and shared an insight with the family. "You know," he said, "today at school I was watching the other guys in my class poking at the girls

The purity of the soul cannot be lost without consent.

and trying to tickle them. I sat there wondering, 'Why don't I ever do anything like that?' Immediately I could hear your voice, Mom, saying, 'Keep your hands off the girls!' Then I knew why I didn't do it!"

I suppose Philip was five when we began repeating that phrase to him. With all our hearts we didn't want our boys to get someone's daughter in trouble. We knew that waiting until they needed such advice, at fifteen or sixteen, would be too late.

We also have warned the boys that any girl who has to paw all over the boys is a girl they want to avoid. It is really disappointing to watch the kids in a Christian high school play a game of volleyball after school, and notice that it is usually the girls who can't leave the boys alone.

If you have thought that childish antics of chasing and kissing are cute and harmless at five, remember they continue and increase at fifteen. If your goal for your children is freedom from syphilis, gonorrhea, and AIDS, then you had better begin doing some old-fashioned warning at eight, nine, and ten years of age. Peer pressure and the media will be pushing your children toward the precipice of immorality. You had better build all the roadblocks you can!

2. Share Scripture with your children this month including the story of Joseph (Genesis 37, 39-50) and Samson (Judges 13–16). These two young men make quite a contrast. In telling the story of Joseph, your explanation to young children need only be that Potiphar's wife wanted Joseph to go to bed with her as if he were her husband, but that Joseph wanted to be morally pure and would not do that.

As for Samson, his beginning in life was as illustrious as John the Baptist's, with an angel foretelling his birth. But Samson's inability to use wisdom in choosing his girlfriends ultimately resulted in his being blinded, imprisoned, and eventually killed. The story of Samson is a useful tool for encouraging your children to seek your counsel when they begin to be interested in a boy or girl. Let them know that you have been there before, and you have some wisdom and insights that can protect them from many unwise choices.

You also can find excellent advice to young men in the first seven chapters of Proverbs. (Interestingly, the adulterous woman is most often described as "flattering with her lips.") A good personal Bible study project for boys would be to see if they can discover what kinds of girls to avoid by reading these chapters.

Use the phrase "moral purity" with your children many times this month and in the coming years. They may not understand its significance for a while, but they will learn early that moral purity is very important.

3. Balance warnings on what to avoid with constructive input on what your children should be looking for in boyfriends and girlfriends. Help them develop a respect for solid character, for that is what they will really need in a life partner. The only way your children will know what to look for in friends is if you teach them about it when they are young. When your children are fifteen it may be too late to try to explain why the class drop-out won't make a good husband—especially if your child is "in love!"

Start now to tell your sons and daughters to be looking for responsibility (Are homework assignments handed in on time?), dependability (Do they bring the snacks for a class party when they promised to?), obedience (Do they obey the teacher? Do they talk rebelliously about their parents' restrictions?), honesty (Do they tell the truth when the teacher asks, "Did you throw that wad of paper?") and perseverance (Do they stick with a difficult math problem or give up when frustrated?).

If you teach these character qualities to your children, they will be able to recognize them—or the lack of them—in their peers. Maybe they will be like the six-year-old who, when asked if he had a girlfriend, said with a grin, "Yes, I like Janie. But I'm watching her character!"

4. Let your children know you are interested in every area of their development. Here are some simple things you can do to help your children adjust to the changes of life and prepare them to listen to your cautions and warnings.

Let your children know that they will be tired as they grow. You may think that sounds silly. How can telling a child to be ready for "the tired's" help him in the trauma of the teen years? Well, it would have helped one of my brothers!

During my kid brother's difficult teen years—when he decided to start wearing a black leather jacket, motorcycle boots, and be a high-school dropout—Mom decided to take him to visit the local police chief. I think part of the idea was that if he thought rebellion was where it was at, he should get acquainted with the local jail!

My brother and the police chief had a long private talk. One of the interesting revelations to come out of that visit was that my brother had been afraid he was going to die! He had grown five or six inches in a couple of years, he was exhausted all the time, and sometimes his heartbeat was irregular.

It never occurred to him to ask, "Why am I tired so much?" Or, "Why does my heart act this way?" Had someone prepared him for these normal effects of adolescence, he and our family might have been spared a good deal of trauma.

I know an active ten- or twelve-year-old can't comprehend the word "tired," but most teens know all about it. I remember our amusement when our youngest at thirteen took his first voluntary Sunday afternoon nap. He emerged from the bedroom afterward shaking his head in disbelief and muttering, "Imagine it! Me! Taking a nap!"

Second, prepare your children ahead of time for changes in their bodies. Do you need a few props to help with this discussion? Here is a simple one: a bottle of deodorant!

Give the bottle to your son or daughter before bed one evening when you have planned time for a talk. Explain to them that many changes are going to be taking place in their bodies soon. Bring out the college textbook again and show them the master gland in their bodies, the pituitary gland, at the base of the cerebrum. (Look in the book's chapter on "Endocrine Glands" or "Hormones.")

Explain that this gland is going to be sending out chemicals called hormones, and that these hormones will cause some changes. One of the changes will be the development of hair under the arms and in the pelvic area. At the same time there will be an increase in sweat production, and since your children don't want to smell bad they will need to start using deodorant when that happens.

Now that is a simple bit of information to share with your children. It is much kinder to do it this way than to inform them one day that they stink! If they do, they probably will think it isn't their fault. After all, they never did before! Adolescents don't understand the changes they experience and really don't know what to do about them. They need your help and guidance.

Other things to prepare your children for include menstruation, the male release of semen at night during teen years ("wet dreams"), voice changes, acne, and so on. Dr. James Dobson's book *Preparing for Adolescence* can be a wonderful springboard for discussion if you will read it to your children. But use it as just that, a springboard for discussion. Don't use it as a substitute for your involvement in your child's learning in this area.

Finally, let your children know they always have your support and love as they mature toward adulthood. And help them understand that as they grow up they move slowly out from under your authority and come directly under God's authority. In light of this, they need to know God's guidelines for moral purity. Most importantly, help them understand that the best way they can prepare for the years ahead is to have a strong personal relationship with Jesus Christ.

Chapter Eleven. Self-Control:
Controlling My Attitudes
and Actions
So They Don't Control Me

The local headlines were emblazoned with the fear of every parent's heart: "Three-Year-Old Missing."

The article explained that a father had taken his three-year-old son with him to look at a friend's new boat. They got on the boat, which was docked along a pier a hundred feet from the river bank, to look around. Then the little fellow pitched a fit in daddy's arms and wanted off. The father gave in to the youngster's tantrum and stood him up on the dock.

When the father emerged from the cabin a minute or so later, the child was nowhere to be seen. A frantic search began. The moments ticked by as the father and his friend checked the boat (had the child gotten back on?) and the waters around the boat (surely he hadn't fallen in?!). Neither man had heard the sound of a splash, and nothing could be seen in the waters around the pier. Yet there hadn't been enough time for the little boy to run down to the parking lot, or for someone to come out and take him.

As seconds stretched into minutes, and minutes into hours, all the distraught father could say was, "I told him to stay right there!" Several days later, the child's lifeless little body was taken from the murky waters.

Sadly, many children could find themselves in similar danger because they are not under control and have not learned much about self-control. Often, parents would consider it absurd to have their children practice sitting on a chair for one minute to learn self-control. Yet this is an exercise that might one day, in a circumstance similar to the story from the paper, save their child's life. It is interesting that we have no qualms about taking the time to teach a puppy to "sit" or "stay," yet we are resistant to teaching our children self-control.

This month we will work on some specific activities centering on self-control. Even if they never actually save your child's life, they will make life happier for your child—and for everyone around him.

SCRIPTURE
The following Scriptures will help you emphasize the importance of self-control.

"He who is slow to anger is better than the mighty, and he who rules his spirit than he who takes a city" (Proverbs 16:32).

"Do not say, 'I will do to him just as he has done to me'" (Proverbs 24:29).

"Do not say, 'I will recompense evil!' Wait for the Lord, and He will save you" (Proverbs 20:22).

"A soft answer turns away wrath, but a harsh word stirs up anger" (Proverbs 15:1).

"Add to your faith . . . self-control" (2 Peter 1:5-6).

"For the weapons of our warfare are . . . mighty in God . . . bringing every thought into captivity" (2 Corinthians 10:4-5).

Consider the first verse. In Bible times, warriors were considered heroes. They were held in as high

Children learn self-control quickest from parents who can control themselves.

esteem as corporate executives or movie stars are today! But this Scripture describes the real super-hero of every age—the one who tops them all—the boy or girl who has self-control!

When I discovered this second Scripture verse I was delighted! If you have ever watched as siblings dodged verbal missiles of "Just you wait and see, I'll get even with you!" or "You'll be sorry when I get you back!" you will be glad for it, too. When children think they have been mistreated, they often become judge, jury, and executioner all in one. Then, after they have administered "justice," they want you to add an additional sentence!

Your children will opt for self-control over revenge only if they know you will do your best to ferret out the truth in their squabbles, despite the myriad accusations flying around. When they know you can be trusted to be fair and just, they usually won't try to right the wrongs done to them. (One warning: children who memorize this particular verse usually can't resist dropping the first three words and quoting the rest of it loudly. But even that typical childish prank can relieve tension and give a comical twist to the conflict.)

The third verse demonstrates why we should exercise self-control instead of revenge: God will be our avenger. While your children are under your care, you are God's minister of justice. Granted, settling your children's many disputes is a task that would overwhelm most court systems! Be encouraged, though, for if you are diligent when your children are small the caseload will lighten as they get older. So make a special effort this month to see that justice prevails. You'll find that your children will soon have confidence in God's—and your—dependability.

As you read the fourth verse, keep in mind that one of the challenges in teaching self-control will be turning "harsh words" into "soft answers." This is a good Scripture to keep on the bulletin board as you work on activities to develop this character quality.

If you have a son or daughter who needs to develop self-control in eating habits, the verse from 2 Peter may be a good verse to use. If you have a child who is beset by fears, the verse from 2 Corinthians can be another opportunity to work with your little worrywart.

One note here: if worrying is a strong personality trait in your child, accept it as a serious challenge. Little people who worry a great deal become big people who find many things to rob them of peace. And they often become old people whose minds are tormented by Satan. Learning to trust God and believe in his love and care is a crucial spiritual discipline. Satan has come to kill, to steal, and to destroy (John 10:10), and one of the things he wants to steal from us and our children is the peace we can have in Christ.

SLOGANS

Here are four slogans you can use as you teach your children about self-control:
- The Strongest Man in the World Is the One Who Can Control Himself.
- A Quiet Voice Is a Sign of Emotions Under Control.

- God Will Help Me Control My Thoughts.
- Self-Control Is a Virtue.

ACTIVITIES

Self-control is a big order even for adults, so be patient as you help your youngsters develop this character

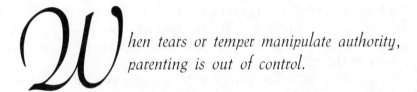

hen tears or temper manipulate authority, parenting is out of control.

quality. Fortunately, there are some activities you and your child can do to work toward this goal even before your child is two.

Between one and two years of age, the "windmill in a windstorm" challenge is a common one. This problem occurs when you are standing talking to a friend, and your eighteen-month-old "jewel" wants down. But, alas, for reasons of life and safety, you do not want her down. So there you stand, almost pummeled to death as your toddler tries to flail, kick, squirm, and shriek her way to the ground. (Oh, the joys of parenthood!)

If, in quieter moments, you have already determined that your child will learn self-control, you will react accordingly when the pressure is on and excuse yourself from the conversation to work with your child. Remember, your child's ability to develop self-control begins with you controlling her. So be sure kicks and screams produce unpleasant rather than pleasant results!

Perhaps your child is a "nursery nuisance," and he is on the verge of being expelled from the church nursery. Contrary to "nursery angels" who are happy to sit and watch other children play—who wouldn't think of taking another child's toy or pulling someone's hair or biting a playmate—your child is into everything and annoying everyone.

If this is the case, realize that a common problem with a nursery nuisance is that he often enjoys the commotion his antics cause. As frustrating as it may be, he probably has no idea of the pain his actions are causing. Too often he won't ever get an idea unless he gets a dose of his own medicine each time he gives it! "An eye for an eye, and a bite for a bite" would certainly have fit my youngest son's interpretation of the golden rule in his pre-school days. "If someone pulls my hair or bites me, I've got to bite them back," he explained. "The Bible says so! It says, 'Do to others as you want them to do to you,' and they did it to me, so they must want me to do it to them!"

If you do not think this "application" of the golden rule is really appropriate, you should come up with some effective way of helping your child understand the pain he causes when he does something unkind.

Fortunately, children outgrow many of these problems. Still, they don't automatically acquire self-control. Without guidance, childish manipulations just take on more sophisticated ploys. This was well illustrated by a young coed in the college freshman speech class I attended years ago. Our assignment was to give a persuasive speech, so she spent fifteen minutes explaining in graphic detail how she had pressured, maneuvered, and wheedled her grandparents into buying her the car she wanted for high school graduation. (She rather resented the professor's subsequent warning to the young men present regarding the treatment they could expect if married to such a woman.)

So begin in the early years to direct your children toward self-control. You will be doing them—and yourself, and those around your children—a great service.

Two to Seven Years Old
1. Bring the "Terrible Tears" under control by rewarding efforts at self-control.

I can remember thinking during my first child's preschool years, "If I can just reach the point where this boy quits crying over every minor incident as if it were a major crisis, maybe I'll make it!" At times it was a great temptation to give in to tears and howls just so deafness would not become an occupational hazard of parenting.

If tears are going to give way to self-control, self-control must be rewarded. Your youngster needs to know that as long as he cries he cannot have what he wants, whether it is an ice cream or a trip to

It is only as you control your child that he will learn to control himself.

Grandma's. There is a difference between saying, "OK, OK, you can have an ice cream—just be quiet!" and saying, "You cannot have an ice cream as long as you cry. You have to stop that." Once the tears are stifled, you can reward the effort at self-control.

There is one problem in this system, however, and it arises when the child's desired object cannot be given. Obviously there will be times when the desires of little hearts cannot and should not be granted. When this happens, the reward for exerting self-control may be that you will read your child a story or spend time together playing a game your child enjoys. Most children would trade anything for undivided parental attention, happily and freely given.

Regardless of the rewards you give, be sure to let your child know that he must stop fussing whether he can have what he wants or not. If your child refuses to stop crying and carrying on, you might consider sending him to his room until he can control himself. Solitude often is a good discipline; it's no fun to carry on without an audience. Or, as hard as it may be, giving your child something to cry about if he continues to scream and fuss to get his way can be an effective deterrent.

2. For a small child, just sitting still for one to two minutes is a wonderful exercise in self-control. If you think sitting on a chair for one minute is no great feat, then you've obviously never tried to get a willful two-year-old to do it!

The first and most important step in this exercise is to decide on your criteria for "sitting" on the chair. Can your child be squatting on it? Standing on it? Lying across the seat? Is he on it as long as one leg is touching the chair? It is up to you, but make your definition clear to the child. Realize that wherever the line is drawn, a battle will be fought.

Second, get two timers with sand in them. This way your child will be able to see "time" passing as the sand trickles from one side of the hourglass to the other. (One note: if your child is small enough, two minutes may be a monumental goal. If this is the case, you can remove the end of the timer and take out some of the sand to make it a one-minute timer—most timers are two- or three-minute timers—then glue the end back on.)

Third, tell your child that any time your criteria for sitting in the chair is not met, the timing starts all over again. (This is why you need the second timer, so you won't have to wait for the sand to get to the other side before beginning again.)

Use affirmative communication with your child as you try this activity. When he squirms, don't ask, "Can't you sit still?" Instead, try telling him, "I know you can sit still—now you're just going to do it."

As parents we need to realize that sitting still isn't just a pointless exercise. It is an important ability for a child to attain. There are times you need your son or daughter to stay put, whether it is by the Sears cashier station as you pay for a pair of shoes or near a busy street. Also, your children will be in school soon and they will be expected to sit for thirty minutes at a time. (Woe to the teacher who gets a youngster like little William, a boy in our son's kindergarten class. During the first weeks of school, we were given daily reports of William's exploits: "William crawled under the table during prayer today," or "When we said the pledge to the flag, William was climbing on top of the bookcase!")

3. Use games to teach emotional control.

Disappointments come to all of us in life and part of maturity is learning to handle them. We had a game I used with our first son to help him learn emotional control. The game had cute plastic trees, and to start playing you hung ten cherries on your tree. The object of the game was to spin the dial and land on a one, two, or three, then pick that many cherries and put them in your little plastic basket. The winner was the one who was first to pick all the cherries off his tree.

However, on that same dial were pictures of a bird and dog. If the dial landed on one of these pictures, that player's basket spilled and all the cherries had to go back on the tree! Oh, what four-year-old agonies we went through if Philip's basket spilled when it was almost full and he was sure he was going to win. What a temptation it was for me to protect him from disappointment and say, "That wasn't a good spin, try again." But I controlled my impulse and helped him through tears and frustration, knowing it was important for him to learn to accept the vicissitudes of life.

Generally, first children and only children especially need to bump into these disappointments of life. Second and third children, however, usually need encouragement to keep at the job and not give up, for their older brothers and sisters will see to it that they toe the line and that spilled baskets are indeed spilled!

4. Your next car trip of several hours can be a good opportunity to help your youngsters learn patience—an important part of self-control.

Have you ever collapsed into the car seat after a frantic rush to get ready for a long trip or vacation, advanced a whole two miles down the road, then had a small voice from the back seat ask, "Are we there yet?"

There you were, heaving a sigh of relief that you had actually gotten on the road, and your angel is already asking that annoying question! While it's true that youngsters have little comprehension of time, they can grasp distances. To help expand their patience and relieve your frazzled nerves, show them a space between your fingers or hands, measuring about two inches for each hour the trip will take. If you have to travel seven hours that day, show them a space of fourteen inches and explain that you have to go that "far." (If you frequently make any trip of an hour or more, show them in inches how "long" that trip takes so they have some standard of comparison.)

Then as the day progresses, show your child how far you have come and how far you have yet to go using your finger or hands. This method seems much more satisfying to children than a perpetual response of, "No! We are not there yet! We still have a long way to go!"

5. Use a "Self-Control Button" on your child's shoulder to help her remember self-control.

Let your youngster color a "button" on paper, then tape it to her shoulder. Or sew a button on a wrist band and let her wear it. When she first puts the button on, take her to the light switch and ask her to turn it on, then off, then on again. Talk about how that switch controls the light, then tell her the two of you will use her "self-control" button to "turn on" self-control. Tell her that when you see behavior that needs to be changed, you will push the button to remind her to practice self-control. If she catches herself in an inappropriate action, she can push the button to remind herself to "turn on" the right behavior.

Eight to Fifteen Years Old

1. Help your children learn self-control in their attitudes.

Attitudes are as important to self-control as actions. While attitudes are more elusive than actions, they can be detected. God has designed our faces as windows to our minds, so you often can tell if your child is thinking defiant or resentful thoughts by his expressions or countenance.

Attitudes affect the "soil" of the soul, much like the roots of azaleas and gardenias influence the soil they grow in. These plants grow best in an acidic soil, and their growth actually increases the acidity of the ground around them. Likewise, resentful attitudes make the soil of the soul sour and provide a fertile area for bitter thoughts to take root.

What can you do about bad attitudes when you detect them? First, you need to remember God's injunction to parents in Ephesians 6:4, "Do not provoke your children to wrath." Then take inventory of your attitudes toward your children. If you have become angry and resentful, you need to ask God—and your children—to forgive you.

Second, don't ignore displays of bitterness or resentment. If you ask your son to carry out the trash and he stomps out of the room complaining about your cruel treatment of him, call him back. Talk about the

S howing self-control with words doesn't mean being silent—it means giving an appropriate response.

situation, reminding him that he has many blessings—home, food, a bed to sleep in, and many hours to play compared to the few minutes of help he is asked to contribute.

If he is still resentful, have him get a piece of paper and write down a list of his chores and how long they take. If he is going to exhibit a bad attitude about his chores, he can spend fifteen minutes talking about the problem instead of the two minutes the task should take. I have often reminded my boys that they could do most chores in half the time they spend complaining about them.

When a child's bad attitude centers around correction, work on the misunderstanding until it has been resolved. In some cases, your child may need some time by himself to work through what he is feeling. So giving him time in his bedroom alone will help clear the atmosphere. Then when you come together again you can work the problem out. But set a time-limit for how long your child will spend in his room, and set a timer for that amount of time with the understanding that you will get together and discuss the issue again when the timer goes off. This will ensure that the situation doesn't just slide by and end up unresolved.

The responses your children give to unhappy circumstances become mental habits, and they will take these "attitude-habits" into adult life. So if your children are allowed to develop negative and bitter attitudes, they will be plagued by them throughout their lives. As one young lady expressed it, "My father made me do what he said, but I could flounce out of the room and be angry in my obedience—he never corrected my attitudes. Now that I'm grown and married, I should be more mature and handle problems with a better attitude. But I act like I did as a child." Little pouters grow up to be big pouters—and no one enjoys being one or having one around.

2. Teach your children self-control in sibling conflicts.

As parents, you play an important role in teaching your children how to handle conflict. You are God's administrator of justice during your children's youth. There are, however, certain standards you should follow when it comes to arbitrating sibling conflicts.

First, let your children know they will get a fair trial in your "court." When you are called upon to deal with disagreements, give that responsibility your undivided attention. Determine whether the sequence of events you are asked to believe is reasonable. When Tommy comes in wailing, "Ryan hit me!" and declares he did nothing to incite his brother, question a bit further. Ask questions like, "You mean you were walking along doing nothing, and Ryan just came up and hit you?" When his answer is a hesitant, "Nooo . . . ," you will know you're on your way to the real story.

Second, if you have a child who claims you always stick up for his brother or sister but never for him, accept his perception as truth to him. For whatever reasons, he is convinced that injustice prevails. This is an unhealthy situation, so you need to treat it sensitively. Pay careful attention to the ways you handle arbitration. Are there times when you automatically assume one child is the culprit? Is it possible that the "innocent" child has begun to expect "diplomatic immunity" and is abusing your confidence in him? Once again, your response and example will be the most effective teachers your children can have. Be willing to evaluate the situation honestly, and make changes where it is necessary.

Finally, don't let "squabble-solving" time turn into a free-for-all. Insist that your children exert self-control and talk one at a time, explaining the problem to you without interrupting each other. And if their views of the problem are contradictory, help them evaluate their own statements for honesty and accuracy.

3. Practice self-control yourself by lowering your voice instead of raising it in frustrating circumstances. And your children will learn self-control in this important area by your example.

Many parents have said, "The kids don't listen unless I raise my voice!" Have you ever tried lowering your voice in an upsetting situation? It is amazing the authority that is conveyed by quiet, deliberate words. It's even more amazing how closely a child will listen to words spoken in a whisper.

After a week of teaching with a bad case of laryngitis, I was convinced a soft voice was better than a loud one. The general classroom noise was cut in half, and the students unconsciously responded to my whispered questions with whispered answers.

To practice this, make a big "First Place" award ribbon to be presented at the evening meal each night this month. Whoever has done the best job of keeping his voice volume under control gets to keep the award to wear the next day. Also, have your child draw a picture of a radio with lips across the front, and a large volume button with the admonition, "Keep the Volume Down."

Chapter Twelve. Generosity: *Freely Sharing My Possessions and My Time*

Christmas!

What a wonderful time of the year to work on the concept of generosity. Sitting around the twinkling lights of the tree listening to Christmas carols provides a perfect setting for telling your children about the greatest example of generosity the world has ever known: the Christ Child, God's gift to mankind.

God's giving us his Son is a wonderful example for you to use through the years to encourage your children to be generous. Fortunately, there will be many opportunities to nourish this character quality during your child's growing-up years. What begins with a struggle to get little pudgy fingers free from a toy culminates in helping a teenager understand that sharing time and ideas are also part of generosity.

But whether it is December or July, the story of God's love and the gift of his Son is the perfect backdrop for working on your child's generosity. In fact, the most memorable reading of the Christmas story I ever heard was during the summer. We were camping in the Blue Ridge Mountains and attended a Sunday morning worship service held at the campsite circle. There was a seminary student in charge of the service, and he read the Christmas story. I think the whole congregation of campers was a bit surprised at the Scripture choice. Then he explained that he chose to read this story because a study of God's great gift can have its greatest impact when it is separated from its usual tinsel and turkey setting. He was right. I, for one, have not forgotten the experience.

SCRIPTURE

The following Scriptures will help you emphasize the importance of generosity.

"Give, and it will be given to you" (Luke 6:38).

"For God so loved . . . that he gave" (John 3:16).

"God loves a cheerful giver" (2 Corinthians 9:7).

"It is more blessed to give than to receive" (Acts 20:35).

The first verse is one with which your children will identify naturally. Perhaps it seems unfortunate to link giving and receiving, but Jesus often put the two together.

There are many Bible stories that illustrate the benefits of generosity. One such story, of the widow of Zarephath, is related in 1 Kings 17:8-16. During the famine of King Ahab's reign, this widow had only enough meal left to fix one more cake for herself and her son. She knew that when the meal was over, they would starve.

Racked as she undoubtedly was by hunger pains, she must have faced quite a challenge when the prophet Elijah came by and asked her to use her pitiful supply of meal to fix him a cake to eat first. Afterward, she could prepare a cake for herself and her son. She probably didn't think there would be any "afterward," but she made a sacrificial gift of that cake in faith. And she and her son reaped the benefits of that faith for the duration of the famine!

Another biblical example is the narrative in Genesis 24. In this chapter we read of Eliezer, who went to search for a wife for his master's son, Isaac. In his journey, Eliezer came to a well and needed water for his camels. It was there that he met Rebekah, who willingly lugged pitcher after pitcher of water to satisfy his parched animals. In performing this act of generosity for a stranger, Rebekah fulfilled the sign Eliezer requested of God to show him the right wife for Isaac.

Another important example is seen in the story of Joseph in Genesis 45. Joseph demonstrated great generosity when he freely forgave his ten brothers, who had tried to kill him years before.

Now consider the second Scripture memory verse from John 3:16. This well-known verse ties together two important concepts: loving and giving.

Children often balk at showing kindness and generosity to those who "don't deserve it." People who fall into this category usually include anyone who has not recently done something nice for the child. You can use John 3:16 to expand your children's understanding about the different kinds of love they can have.

The love that prompted God to give his Son centered on the need and happiness of the ones for whom the gift was given. In other words, God gave us his Son not because of any love and kindness we had shown him, but because we needed a Savior. As your children mature, their giving should develop an element of generosity that enables them to give without first receiving.

The story of the Good Samaritan recounted in Luke 10:34 is an interesting story to use in illustrating this principle. You can read it at bedtime or in family devotions. If you explain the antagonism that existed between the Samaritans and the Jews, you will help your children understand that even the disliked child on the block or in the classroom deserves their kindness and generosity. Ultimately, learning the art of unselfish giving will make your children better people.

Such giving is the stuff of which modern heroes are made. Consider the Air Florida jet that crashed into the Potomac River moments after take-off one winter not long ago. Only five of the seventy-nine passengers survived that air tragedy. During rescue operations, a middle-aged man was seen repeatedly passing the lifeline to fellow passengers who were clinging to the broken fuselage of the plane. He was more concerned with saving others than himself. Then, before the rescue crew could make a last trip for him, he lost his grip on the plane and disappeared beneath the icy waters. This man was a true example of selfless giving, and of Christ's words in John 15:13: "Greater love has no one than this, than to lay down one's life for [another]."

As you read the third Scripture verse, 2 Corinthians 9:7, try to remember if you've ever had the privilege of knowing someone who was genuinely and spontaneously generous. When I meet a person like this I am reminded that we were made in God's image. People who radiate attractive qualities such as friendliness, kindness, or generosity are just reflecting God's attributes. It is intriguing to think for a moment about what Adam must have been like before the fall! Made in the image of God, he embodied in one individual all those admirable qualities we only glimpse here and there throughout humanity.

People who possess the glowing ember of generosity are inspiring examples for the rest of us. Apparently one result from the fall of man is that we have become naturally selfish and inclined to focus on ourselves. But such a focus will never bring happiness. Only through giving in love can we find real joy.

The final verse, Acts 20:35, is hardly believable for small children since they generally are still deep in the egocentric stage of life. Getting is everything to little children; giving often is devastating. Most people leave childish self-centeredness behind as they mature and discover the joy of giving. There are those, however, who never learn the truth of Acts 20:35.

In our ministry, my husband and I have encountered both kinds of people. I remember one elderly couple who attended our congregation for about a year. They received invitations to dinner, cards when sick, and were even given a party in their honor. In many different ways they were showered with special kindness and encouragement from their church family.

All these things seemed lost in the old gentleman's expanse of need. He had been an only child and his wife seemed to have spent their fifty-plus years of marriage catering to him, seeing that he had his way.

The tragedy of a self-centered life is that focusing on self makes it impossible for a person to gain the happiness he seeks.

Yet none of this seemed to make him more generous to others. Instead, it only reinforced his self-centered focus. No matter how much was done for him, it was never enough. He finally left the church, declaring it a group of unfriendly people.

His pew was soon filled by another senior citizen named Rusty. This man was soon busy trying to help on church projects and doing things for others. The cards he received in times of sickness were amazing treasures to him. The invitations to dinner and the phone calls of concern he received overwhelmed him. His small cup of expectation often overflowed with the kindness of the congregation.

God has said it is more blessed to give than to receive because he knows man was originally designed in his likeness. We reap inner joy and satisfaction when we bring happiness to others, just as God rejoices to give good gifts to his children. Share with your children often this month the truth that the joy of giving is greater than any pleasure they can feel from receiving.

SLOGANS

Here are several interesting slogans you can use to teach your children about generosity:

- Generosity Begins Today.
- Generosity Is Contagious.
- Jesus Says Share.

As the first slogan states, today is the day to begin being generous. Have you ever heard the "If I were rich, I would give . . ." stories? Here is one such story:

> *Joe and Sam were walking down the road. Joe was complaining to Sam about being poor. Sam felt very sympathetic and exclaimed, "You know, Joe, I wish I could help you. Why, if I had a hundred dollars, I'd give you fifty!"*
>
> *Joe was impressed with his friend's professed generosity. Sam went on to declare, "In fact, if I had fifty dollars, I'd give you twenty-five."*
>
> *"You're a real friend, Sam," Joe said. "If you had ten dollars would you give me five dollars?"*
>
> *"That's not fair, Joe!" Sam said. "You* know *I have ten dollars!"*

You can share this simple little story with your children during the month. It is amusing, yet it underscores the truth that real generosity begins today by sharing what we have—not tomorrow, with vague promises of what we would do if we had an abundance.

Jesus commends a widow in Luke 21:4 who gave generously though she was poor. (To make this Scripture more real to your children, you may want to spend a few moments with them imagining what this widow's life was like and what prompted her to give to the Temple treasury.)

The second slogan shows that unpleasant things such as colds and measles aren't the only things that can be "caught." Good things like kindness and generosity are contagious, too. Even small children understand that smiling at baby brother or sister usually gets them a smile in return. Perhaps if you explain this simple object lesson to your children it will help them see that if they are kind and share, others around them may "catch" the generosity "germ" and learn to share, too.

The concept of the last slogan runs throughout the Scriptures. In Matthew 5:40-42, Jesus tells us to be willing to give even beyond what we are asked, and to not turn away from those who want to share something with us. This particular slogan was one of our boys' favorites—especially when someone else had something they wanted!

Generosity begins today by sharing what we have, not in the vague tomorrows by planning to share what may never be ours.

ACTIVITIES

There are few dads or moms who have escaped having a baby bottle held to their lips, or missed being offered an animal cracker held tightly in a chubby fist as their child looks up at them with a dimpled smile and sparkling eyes. At such moments, parental thoughts do not usually center on budding generosity. But such is the beginning of generous impulses.

Should you find yourself on the receiving end of your child's offering, do not recoil. Instead, play along with your baby's game by pretending to indulge, then offer the "dainties" back again. This gives your child the opportunity to develop generosity in his earliest days, and can form the foundation for sharing when he is three and four years old.

If your child doesn't initiate sharing, you can encourage it by giving him things specifically for that purpose. For example, give him two cookies, then either ask for one back again or ask him to give one to his brother or sister. You can broaden the scope of this exercise by giving your child two toys with instructions to give one to a playmate. Of course, your role is to be encouraging and to follow through and see that the gift is given—and to enforce the rules that if the child doesn't share he will lose both treasures.

Two to Seven Years Old

1. A trip to the grocery store this month may be enlivened by turning it into a "Share-a-Smile Safari." As your youngsters ride over the rugged terrain in a grocery cart, they can see how many smiles they can capture by giving out smiles of their own. Children who initially learn to be generous with intangible things, such as a smile, often find it easier later on to share the more tangible things, such as a toy.

2. Act the part of another child in different activities and insist that your child share with you, just as any other child would. Let your child practice generosity by giving him a small bag of popcorn or peanuts, then let him divvy them up in the "one for you, one for me" fashion.

3. Something as simple as specific guidelines for dividing up toys can prevent sibling conflict and teach children about sharing. When the objects in question are inherently different and vary in desirability, as with toy cars or dolls, parcel them out by letting the children alternately take turns choosing which ones they want. (You may want to flip a coin to see who goes first, just to be sure everyone feels you have been fair.)

4. If you have several preschool children who share the same toys, you may find these techniques from nursery schools helpful. When a child brings a new toy from home for "show and tell," all the children sit in a row on the rug. Then a real production is made of the toy being passed slowly from hand to hand, and each child has a minute to "play" with it. This helps eliminate the free-for-all that too often occurs when a new toy arrives. This technique may also be helpful for Christmas day, when a number of new toys come on the scene.

5. A minute timer may help you maintain your sanity as you try to teach generosity. This way you can set up a time limit for turns with a toy in advance. The ringing of the timer will let the child—and you—know that a turn has ended. This also will end conflicts over one child getting to do or play with something longer than another.

I don't remember seeing any such timers during my childhood, but I know my parents understood the principle. One Christmas in particular stands out. We four children—two girls and two boys—received shiny new bikes. There was one bike for the two boys, and one for the two girls. I remember that Christmas day better than most others because of the conflict that resulted over those bikes.

What a time we had fussing about whose turn it was to ride, and who was getting the longest turn! My folks finally ended up decreeing that each child had a fifteen-minute time limit per turn per bike!

Timing turns may not be the highest level of sharing, but it does give a child a chance to develop patience while she waits for her turn. And it makes life much more bearable for Mom and Dad!

6. Another activity this month is planning a "Praise-Day Party" each week. Instead of having your children eat cake and get presents as they would at a birthday party, this will be a time for them to *give* gifts of encouragement and praise to family members and playmates. A tally of praise-gifts given can be kept on a sheet of paper on the side of the refrigerator.

Eight to Fifteen Years Old

As your children mature they will be able to understand the more abstract aspects of generosity—namely sharing the glory of an accomplishment or an idea.

1. *The Christmas Carol* by Charles Dickens, about that miserly old Ebenezer Scrooge, would be an enjoyable tale for you to read as a family this month. It is a charming and pointed commentary on the tragedy of stinginess.

Aesop's Fables also are delightful tales to share with your children while they still enjoy having you read to them. Many of these stories contrast selfishness and generosity, and encourage the nobler qualities.

2. Watch the newspaper during the month for stories about generosity. Share what you find with the family at dinner or at a family talk time.

3. With Christmas approaching, the special project for the month might be helping your children make handmade gifts for different family members. Such gifts might include a letter of appreciation to Grandma and Grandpa; a coaster for Dad's coffee mug; an onion-shaped cutting board for Mom; or a rock paperweight with a smiley face or other pictures painted on it.

4. Now is a good time for your family to experiment with promissory coupons as gifts. Make up your own coupons for such things as, "A hug at the end of a weary day," or "Good for half of my next Popsicle." Regardless of the occasion, these coupons are a creative way of doing some heartfelt sharing that doesn't have to include materialism.

5. One of the most valuable aids for teaching generosity is parental example. Children are keenly aware of whether generosity is something you believe in enough to practice. See that you willingly share smiles, words of encouragement, or even part of a candy bar.

Appendix:
Scripture Verses

CHAPTER 2

"*A man who refuses to admit his mistakes can never be successful. But if he confesses and forsakes them, he gets another chance*" (Proverbs 28:13, TLB).

"*He who conceals his sins does not prosper, but whoever confesses and renounces them finds mercy*" (Proverbs 28:13, NIV).

"*God delights in those who keep their promises, and abhors those who don't*" (Proverbs 12:22, TLB).

"*The Lord detests lying lips, but he delights in men who are truthful*" (Proverbs 12:22, NIV).

CHAPTER 3

"*If you refuse to discipline your son, it proves you don't love him; for if you love him you will be prompt to punish him*" (Proverbs 13:24, NIV).

"*Don't fail to correct your children; discipline won't hurt them! . . . Punishment will keep them out of hell*" (Proverbs 23:13-14, TLB).

"*The Lord disciplines those he loves, and he punishes everyone he accepts as a son*" (Hebrews 12:6, NIV).

"*He who spares the rod hates his son, but he who loves him is careful to discipline him*" (Proverbs 13:24, NIV).

"*Scolding and spanking a child helps him to learn. Left to himself, he brings shame to his mother*" (Proverbs 29:15, TLB).

"Punishment that hurts chases evil from the heart" (Proverbs 20:30, TLB).

"The character of even a child can be known by the way he acts—whether what he does is pure and right" (Proverbs 20:11, TLB).

"Even a child is known by his actions, by whether his conduct is pure and right" (Proverbs 20:11, NIV).

"To obey is better than sacrifice . . . For rebellion is like the sin of divination, and arrogance like the evil of idolatry" (1 Samuel 15:22-23, NIV).

"Obedience is far better than sacrifice. [God] is much more interested in your listening to him than in your offering. . . . For rebellion is as bad as the sin of witchcraft" (1 Samuel 15:22-23, TLB).

CHAPTER 4

"The character of even a child can be known by the way he acts—whether what he does is pure and right" (Proverbs 20:11, TLB).

"Even a child is known by his actions, by whether his conduct is pure and right" (Proverbs 20:11, NIV).

"A lazy fellow [child] is a pain to his employers [parents]—like smoke in their eyes" (Proverbs 10:26, TLB).

"As vinegar to the teeth and smoke to the eyes, so is a sluggard to those who send him" (Proverbs 10:26, NIV).

"Unless you are honest in small matters, you won't be in large ones. If you cheat even a little, you won't be honest with greater responsibilities" (Luke 16:10, TLB).

"Whoever can be trusted with very little can also be trusted with much" (Luke 16:10, NIV).

"Have you considered my servant Job? There is no one on earth like him; he is blameless and upright, a man who fears God and shuns evil" (Job 1:8, NIV).

CHAPTER 5
"A happy face means a glad heart; a sad face means a breaking heart" (Proverbs 15:13, TLB).

"A happy heart makes the face cheerful, but heartache crushes the spirit" (Proverbs 15:13, NIV).

"No matter how much we see, we are never satisfied; no matter how much we hear, we are not content" (Ecclesiastes 1:8, TLB).

"The eye never has enough of seeing, nor the ear its fill of hearing" (Ecclesiastes 1:8, NIV).

CHAPTER 6
"Whatever your hand finds to do, do it with all your might" (Ecclesiastes 9:10, TLB).

"Whatever you do, do well" (Ecclesiastes 9:10, NIV).

"Do everything for the glory of God, even your eating and drinking" (1 Corinthians 10:31, TLB).

"Whatever you do, do it all for the glory of God" (1 Corinthians 10:31, NIV).

CHAPTER 7
"Honor the Lord by giving him the first part of all your income" (Proverbs 3:9, TLB).

"Honor the Lord with your wealth, with the firstfruits of all your crops" (Proverbs 3:9, NIV).

"Bring all the tithes into the storehouse so that there will be food enough in my Temple; if you do, I will open up the windows of heaven for you and pour out a blessing so great you won't have room enough to take it in!" (Malachi 3:10, TLB).

"Bring the whole tithe into the storehouse, that there may be food in my house. Test me in this," says the Lord Almighty, *"and see if I will not throw open the floodgates of heaven and pour out so much blessing that you will not have room enough for it"* (Malachi 3:10, NIV).

"If you give to the poor, your needs will be supplied! But a curse upon those who close their eyes to poverty" (Proverbs 28:27, TLB).

"He who gives to the poor will lack nothing, but he who closes his eyes to them receives many curses" (Proverbs 28:27, NIV).

CHAPTER 9

"Timely advice is as lovely as gold apples in a silver basket" (Proverbs 25:11, TLB).

"A word aptly spoken is like apples of gold in settings of silver" (Proverbs 25:11, NIV).

CHAPTER 10

"Your body is the home of the Holy Spirit" (1 Corinthians 6:19, TLB).

"Your body is a temple of the Holy Spirit" (1 Corinthians 6:19, NIV).

"If you can find a truly good wife, she is worth more than precious gems! Her husband can trust her, and she will richly satisfy his needs" (Proverbs 31:10-11, TLB).

"A wife of noble character who can find? She is worth far more than rubies. Her husband has full confidence in her and lacks nothing of value" (Proverbs 31:10-11, NIV).

CHAPTER 11

"It is better to be slow-tempered than famous; it is better to have self-control than to control an army" (Proverbs 16:32, TLB).

"Better a patient man than a warrior, a man who controls his temper than one who takes a city" (Proverbs 16:32, NIV).

"Don't say, 'Now I can pay him back for all his meanness to me!'" (Proverbs 24:29, TLB).

"Do not say, 'I'll do to him as he has done to me'" (Proverbs 24:29, NIV).

"Don't repay evil for evil. Wait for the Lord to handle the matter" (Proverbs 20:22, TLB).

"Do not say, 'I'll pay you back for this wrong!' Wait for the Lord, and he will deliver you" (Proverbs 20:22, NIV).